WHO'S DOING THE WORK?

WHO'S DOING THE WORK?

Jan Burkins and Kim Yaris

HOW TO SAY LESS SO READERS CAN DO MORE

Foreword by
Joan Moser
of *"The 2 Sisters"*

Stenhouse Publishers
Portland, Maine

Stenhouse Publishers
www.stenhouse.com

Library of Congress Cataloging-in-Publication Data

Names: Burkins, Jan Miller, 1968- author. | Yaris, Kim, author.
Title: Who's doing the work? : how to say less so your readers can do more /
    Jan Burkins and Kim Yaris.
Description: Portland, Maine : Stenhouse Publishers, 2016. | Includes
    bibliographical references.
Identifiers: LCCN 2015043477 (print) | LCCN 2016004161 (ebook) | ISBN
    9781625310750 (pbk. : alk. paper) | ISBN 9781625310767 (ebook)
Subjects: LCSH: Reading (Elementary) | Oral reading. | Group reading. |
    Guided reading.
Classification: LCC LB1573 .B874 2016 (print) | LCC LB1573 (ebook) | DDC
    372.4--dc23
LC record available at http://lccn.loc.gov/2015043477

Cover and interior design by Lucian Burg, Lu Design Studios, Portland, ME
www.ludesignstudios.com

Manufactured in the United States of America

PRINTED ON 30% PCW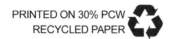
RECYCLED PAPER

22 21 20 19 18 17 16   9 8 7 6 5 4 3

Dedication

For Daisy

CONTENTS

Foreword

By Joan Moser

This is a book that needed to be written—for teachers, coaches, administrators, or anyone who cares about children of all ages.

I am returning to the sport of golf after a lengthy respite. Picking up clubs again brought back the familiar albeit frustrating feeling of learning something new. I was fortunate enough to find a golf coach skilled at assessing, diagnosing, and instructing everything from swing technique to course management. His coaching was so effective that, during our first meeting, I was hitting the ball akin to my golf days of the past. Alas, the success was short lived, for as soon as I ventured off without my trusty coach I was back to square one; even more concerning, all of a sudden I questioned whether or not I could ever golf successfully on my own.

Lamenting my poor play at our second meeting, I found that the lesson transpired differently. Each time I struck the ball poorly, I looked to Coach for swing-by-swing feedback, the suggestions and tips he had provided in the first session. But this time, each imploring look I gave was met with a smile and silence. I battled the frustration bubbling up within me as I asked him what I should do. He responded with four simple words, "What could you try?"

Those four words completely changed the outcome of the coaching session. They required me to pause and think about the strategies he had taught me. He was asking me to do the work of problem solving, rather than relying on him to do it for me. Red in the face, I had to admit I really had no idea what to do. Yes, I had taken the feedback he provided and put it into immediate action during our first lesson, but I was unable to replicate the strategies away from his coaching.

Immediately I recognized that I had come to rely on him to do the work for me and, as a result, put myself in a position of being utterly helpless. Simultaneously he indicated that he had changed his goal for me. Rather than to merely improve my game with his coaching, his new goal was for me to be able to problem solve, self-correct, and think through what I was doing on my own, away from him. In other words, to have me do the work first, followed by his selective and focused feedback.

By now you may be wondering how my golfing is connected to this book that *needed to be written.* As you may have figured out, my coach is also a teacher. We have had many conversations about everything from effective instructional techniques to guided practice. After our first few sessions together, our dialogues shifted to the many things we do as educators that are automatic, with little clear thought to their effectiveness. Some of these practices are hardwired into our DNA (for example, doing a summary of the text for students before reading, or preteaching vocabulary). For Coach, it meant he was hardwired to offer suggestions and tips after each and every one of my swings of the club.

Some of our teaching techniques may be a result of the education system over-correcting itself, going from one swing of the pendulum to the next. In some cases we may have participated in practices that, deep down, we knew were not in the best interest of students. (Consider the way we give children extremely hard text and assume that, with enough scaffolding, they will be able to read it.) In many recent cases these practices, whether hardwired or learned, appear to have been taken to the extreme. Teachers are being asked to do more and more talking, in the way of explaining, modeling, and instructing, while providing students even less time to do the actual reading and writing. When we function on autopilot, it becomes difficult to gain perspective or clearly reflect on our practices, which results in instruction that is less than effective.

Coach articulated that when he heard I didn't think I would ever be able to golf without him at my side, it surprised him into awareness. He became acutely conscious of the fact that he was teaching on autopilot rather than being mindful and reflective of what he had assessed as the specific needs of the person in front of him.

In their book *Decisive: How to Make Better Choices in Life and Work* (Crown Business, 2013), Chip and Dan Heath talk about a "tripwire" that can jolt people out of autopilot and into awareness. Coach and I talked about the need for educators to have this mechanism—something to make us pause, step back, gain better perspective, and clearly reflect on our practices, all in the effort to course-correct and better meet the needs of our students.

I am delighted to say that the book you hold in your hands has been that trip-wire for me. From its opening pages where you meet Daisy and her teacher, you will see the positive and negative power of the language we sometimes use with automaticity when working with students. Reading this book has provided the tripwire for some of the language and instructional practices I have used with students. I heard some of myself in Daisy's well-intended teacher, and saw some of my own students who, like Daisy, became disengaged and dependent on me.

As the creators of the Daily 5 and CAFE systems, my sister Gail Boushey and I have been devoted to the beliefs and practices of fostering independence and agency in students. *Who's Doing the Work?* clearly aligns with these practices and beliefs. This book does not advocate the simple idea of the teacher doing less. Rather, it is a guide to being intentional about *what we do less of.*

The message so beautifully conveyed by the authors of this book is the desire for students of all levels to become agentive readers. Jan and Kim have provided tripwires that empower us to reflect and course-correct our own language and practices. Their message is delivered in a way that leads to fostering students in our classrooms who understand what they are capable of (which is often more than they—or the teacher—think).

I want to believe that all people involved with the education of our students are attempting to make the best decisions because they love and care about children and want the best for them and our future society. Yet given the current state of education, it is clear we all need a tripwire or a touchstone to remind us and guide us to make decisions based on best practice and students' individual needs, so we can raise children who are able to work independently. Therefore I stand in the place of *This is a book that needed to be written* and now say to you, *This is a book that needs to be read.*

Acknowledgments

In R. J. Palacio's book *Wonder* (2012), Mr. Browne opens the school year by having his students write down this precept: "When given the choice between being right or being kind, choose kind" (48). We try to live by this precept but, when it comes to working with a publishing house, we want to work with people who are also right!

We are deeply grateful that the lovely people at Stenhouse Publishers have perfected the beautiful and paradoxical art of being both kind *and* right. They know how to gracefully support writers as they turn general ideas into finished books, thoughtfully attending to their writing needs (and their emotional needs) throughout the process.

We cannot describe how much we love Dan Tobin. He is the smartest nice man we know (or should we say nicest smart man?). Dan, thank you for believing in our project.

Maureen Barbieri, our editor, faithfully offered wise advice in ways that communicated her affection for us and her confidence in our vision for *Who's Doing the Work?* Thank you, Maureen. Without fail, every bit of your advice made this book better.

Jay Kilburn's willingness to marry our blurry design vision with his design prowess gave us a book cover and interior design that we love. Meanwhile, Erin Trainer and Chris Downey, copyeditors extraordinaire, lovingly and tediously deliberated over every sentence of our manuscript. Their humor and patience made our work more fun and our book better.

For us, navigating marketing and social media is like rowing a dinghy during a hurricane. Chuck Lerch and Zsofia McMullin make these waters feel far less tumultuous, and we sincerely appreciate the work they do to make the complexities of marketing easier to navigate.

We want to conclude our special thanks to the Stenhouse team with a shout-out to Chandra Lowe, who does a mind-bogglingly amazing job of remembering everything. Nobody—and we seriously mean nobody—is as good as Chandra at managing details. Chandra, thank you for using your superpower on our behalf.

We deeply appreciate the wise and courageous Joan Moser, who wrote the foreword for *Who's Doing the Work?* Joan, thank you for dedicating your time and intention to our project. We have tremendous respect for the way you work and the results of your efforts, and are honored that you have lent your talents to our book.

Who's Doing the Work? is the product of years of work with many teachers in many classrooms across the country. We want to thank all of the teachers and administrators who have welcomed us into their classrooms and schools, allowed us to share our ideas, and helped us to refine our thinking. We'd especially like to thank Jared Bloom, Alison Bruno, Anthony Ciccarelli, Melody Croft, Vito D'Elia, Pam Fine, Melissa Graham, Adam Kurtz, Annie Michaelian, Chara Moore, April Poprilo, Xernona Thomas, Elissa Toubin, and Tricia Wilkinson.

We are lovingly supported by educators who make our work richer and better. To Amy Brennan, Trevor Bryan, Dani Burtsfield, Jill DeRosa, Justin Dolci, Donna Donner, JoAnne Duncan, Bob Fecho, Julieanne Harmatz, Jenn Hayhurst, Kathryn Hoffman-Thompson, Fran McVeigh, Joan Moser, Erica Pecorale, Jennifer Sniadecki, Peggy Terrell, Kari Yates, and Mary Howard—thank you for always pushing our thinking, for helping us be our best selves, and for making our lives rich and joyful.

We also want to offer a special thank you to Brenda Power, who gave us the opportunity to explore some of these ideas on Choice Literacy before they made it into this book.

Finally, *Who's Doing the Work?* wouldn't have been possible without the support, encouragement, and cooperation of our families. We'd like to give a collective hug to the people who share our homes and our hearts, and who loved and buoyed us through the months of writing this book. Thank you Nate, Duncan, Christopher, Natie, Victor, Craig, Matthew, and Nathan. We promise to play more *Monopoly* and bake more cookies now that the book is finished.

What Painting, Housework, and Designing Sofas Can Teach Us About Developing Agentive Readers

*I*n a kindergarten classroom in New York, Kim watches a teacher work with a group of students. The teacher is trying to do less of the work for students for the first time. One of the young, novice readers works very hard to read a line of text that includes the word seaweed, a big word for a beginning reader. The teacher lets him deliberate without interrupting or leading him, and he manages to figure out the word. Once he says "seaweed," however, he immediately looks at the teacher for confirmation. Rather than telling him that he has figured out the word—as self-checking is a critical skill that students must learn to do themselves—the teacher waits as the student stares at her and refuses to turn the page. After several long moments, the principal, who is also watching the lesson, eventually leans forward and tells the student to turn the page. But he won't—not until his teacher tells him whether or not he has read the word correctly.

In a small room in a school in the Midwest, three third-grade boys have been pulled from their regular classroom for a second dose of guided reading. The boys have been together since kindergarten, where their struggles with reading were identified early. The school's literacy coach is understandably concerned and asks Jan for her opinion. Jan decides to teach the boys a guided reading lesson to get a better sense of their reading processes. The boys are reading from a level H book (Fountas and Pinnell 1996) and are working substantially "below grade level." From the book room, Jan selects a text about two boys caught in a storm, which she thinks will interest them. After introducing herself at the start of the lesson and engaging the boys in some small talk to put them at ease, Jan distributes the text. Rather than summarizing it for the boys, she says, "We have this new book to read

1

today. What should we do to get started?" The boys sit in silence for several seconds. Jan repeats the question: "Well, what are we going to do to figure out this book?" Another long pause. The students look at each other, at the table, and back at Jan. Finally, one boy raises his hand, slowly, and responds with a statement that is really a question: "We could open it?"

In the 1960s, Martin Seligman, the father of positive psychology, discovered that dogs who were subjected to electric shocks while they were locked in cages did not later try to escape similar shocks when their cages were wide open (Seligman and Maier 1967). These dogs were so accustomed to *not* having a choice that when they really *did* have a choice, they didn't recognize it. Ultimately, these poor dogs were trained to have a fixed mindset (Dweck 2006; Johnston 2012), or in other words, they learned helplessness.

Of course, we aren't comparing reading instruction to experiments on animals; learned helplessness can happen around just about anything—from keeping a clean house to finding a job. Rather, we are comparing the way the dogs in the experiments reacted—helplessly—when they were later given a choice, much like the readers in the stories above.

When people spend time in situations where they have little or no power, they become unable to recognize when they actually *do* have power. The aforementioned instances of students' learned helplessness make us wonder about some of our traditional approaches to reading instruction, which develop readers who wait for us to make decisions for them, even when we put them in control.

As described in the stories that open this introduction, the obvious work of confirming a word, turning a page, or even opening a book leaves students at a real loss when they are accustomed to reading instruction that includes statements such as the following:

- "Before you start reading, turn to page 3 and point to the word in bold. That word is *individual*."
- "Turn to page 7 and look at the picture. What do you notice about where the dog is hiding?"
- "Get your mouth ready."

In the age of high-stakes testing and high accountability, scaffolding has become a euphemism for the teacher doing much of the work. Throughout read-aloud, shared reading, guided reading, and independent reading—which we refer to throughout this book as the *instructional contexts*—we have unwittingly assumed too much of the important work—telling students when to think, when they are having difficulties, how to resolve a problem, and even when to turn the page. Not only that, but in telling them when to do something, we tell them *not* to act until we prompt them. Educators everywhere are discovering that such support isn't sustainable, as students plateau, become unengaged, and demonstrate less proficiency rather than more.

In our work as consultants in schools, we regularly hear the same lament: "We are working so hard to help our students improve, but no matter what we do, they are not making the progress we want them to!" In these conversations, teachers' pain is palpable. They want to know what to do. Surprisingly, we want them to *do* less.

How Learning to Read Is Not Like Painting a Ceiling

In construction, a *scaffold* is a temporary structure, usually a platform, which gives a worker access to space or tasks that would otherwise be out of reach. Painters use scaffolds when painting ceilings, and builders use scaffolds when refacing multiple-story buildings. However, for painters and construction workers, when the scaffolding is removed, they are no longer able to reach their work. If their next job requires them to replace a window on the sixteenth floor, they must set up scaffolding once again. The scaffolding on one job does not make them better equipped for doing similar work *without* scaffolding. This is where the scaffolding metaphor as it is used in reference to teaching and learning falls apart for us.

How much support to offer students while they negotiate texts, particularly those of increasing complexity, is a concern reverberating through the educational community. "Provide scaffolding" has been education's blanket answer to many of the most complex teaching and learning situations. As Pea (2004) writes, "The concept of scaffolding has become so broad in its meanings in the field of educational research and the learning sciences that it has become unclear in its significance" (423). First introduced by Wood, Bruner, and Ross in 1976, and later shaped by Vygotsky's "zone of proximal development" (1978), *scaffolding* has evolved to become all things to all educators. Consider the following contexts where scaffolding, as most educators know and understand it, is common:

- Students lack the background knowledge to read a piece of historical fiction about the Revolutionary War, so the teacher presents a brief synopsis of the time period and introduces period terminology that is likely to stump the readers.
- A new text contains the words *flax*, *awl*, *fiber*, and *trousers* in one passage. The teacher begins the lesson by writing these words on the board and providing students with an example or definition of each.
- The first chapter of a story introduces Mr. Hawthorne and Mrs. Hawthorne; their children, Pamela, Stuart, and Delilah; and their nanny, Mrs. Robertson. Before the children read, the teacher spends time explaining that the chapter has several characters. The teacher also gives the students a piece of paper with the list of character names and roles, instructing students to look for clues in the text that will help them understand the characters and their actions.

While we aren't saying that teachers should never support students in these ways, we *are* saying that, if we want students to use strategies independently, we must question the ways our "scaffolding" may get in the way.

Who's Doing the (House) Work?

We both travel a lot and, between us, we have six sons. Initially, when we left town, many of the household responsibilities that are usually in our charge simply fell by the wayside. We finally realized that, in order to help our husbands, who manage hearth and home in our frequent absences, and to teach our sons responsibility, we needed to step up our expectations of the children as contributing members of our households. Informed by our teaching experience, we set in place procedures and routines and thoroughly taught the children how to do them. We coached them on unloading the dishwasher, sorting laundry, and vacuuming.

We soon realized, however, that we had made a mistake. We didn't really teach our sons *when* to employ these strategies. When we woke them up in the mornings, we said, "Don't forget to do your chores," or "You have to unload the dishwasher before breakfast." Although they knew how to unload the dishwasher, they didn't know how to *choose* to unload the dishwasher. Rather than watch the trash to notice when it needed taking out, they waited for us to prompt them. Yes, they knew how to take out the trash, but as you might have guessed, when we left town again, the "routines" ground to a startlingly quick halt, illustrating that they were not routine at all. Because we had built ourselves into the process, scaffolding heavily, our sons had no ownership, or agency, of their routines.

Similarly, education's current approach to scaffolding readers supports students in ways that eliminate much, if not all, of the decision making for them. Consequently, the scaffold in one reading experience does not translate to independent work as often as it seems it should. When students wobble (Fecho 2013) in recognizing a word, we swoop in with "Get your mouth ready"—the teaching equivalent of "Unload the dishwasher before breakfast." When they hiccup while explaining what a word in a sentence means, we quickly guide them to reread the part that restates the meaning of the word. We do a lot of digging into text in order to eliminate confusion (and responsibility) for students, and our lesson plans are testimony to how much of the work we are planning to do.

However, the practice of using specific prompts such as "Get your mouth ready," "Does that make sense?" and "Does that sound right" systematically overrides students' self-monitoring systems by giving them less and less that *doesn't* make sense. We eliminate their need to identify the nature of the problem, and in turn, students don't learn that confusion is their clue to look more closely at text.

If, after the lesson, readers are no better equipped to encounter a similar text *without* our scaffolding, then we haven't given them much that can transfer. They are likely always to need us to pick out the hard words, explain the character structure, and orient them to the plot, just as our children need us to tell them when to take out the trash. Why are we surprised when we confer with an independent reader who is rushing past unknown words and reading for superficial understandings? Rather than creating independence, scaffolding in the traditional way can create a process that *requires* continued support. Teachers become permanent scaffolds, and students learn helplessness.

Next Generation Reading Instruction

We use the term *next generation* in reference to conventional practices that have naturally evolved as educators respond to student needs. Next generation reading instruction requires us to scrutinize our lessons through a lens of student independence/dependence and involves identifying places where we are assuming student work that students could do if we let them. Tasks like those described earlier, such as preteaching vocabulary or summarizing the main idea of the text before students read it, are called into question when we notice the ways they often create dependence in students. Here are a few questions that can guide us as we move toward next generation reading instruction:

- Can students identify the areas of the work that need their attention? *Ex: Rather than preteach vocabulary words and point out parts that might be hard in a text, have students work in pairs to skim the text and discuss how they will manage what they anticipate will be difficult for them.*
- Can students decide the type of strategy they need to use or work they need to do to understand a text? *Ex: Rather than tell students to work on inferring with a particular text, tell them to read a new text and then let them suggest a strategy and talk about how it did or didn't work and why.*
- Can students self-monitor their understanding and identify the areas of the text that they do not understand? *Ex: Rather than introduce a text by giving students a summary or telling them ahead of time which parts of the text are "tricky," thus preempting that trickiness, have them work in pairs to identify the parts of the text that require clarification.*
- Can students share their thinking about the strategies that work for them? *Ex: Rather than tell students what to do first, second, and third to understand a text, let them work with partners to see what they can figure out and to create anchor charts that list their strategies.*

Though there are occasions when it makes sense to approach text in more traditional ways, next generation reading instruction gives students decision-making power, letting them practice the messy work of figuring out what to do and when to do it. By reframing difficulty as opportunity, children begin to see the connection between their effort and their success. We call this *productive effort*—hard work that results in success rather than frustration. Carefully deciding *how* to scaffold student learning is a key to optimizing the benefits of this effort, thus increasing the likelihood that the skills and strategies we teach transfer when children are working independently. Next generation reading instruction is responsive to students' needs. Rather than teachers always making the decisions about what to teach and when it should be taught, instructional decisions are made as a result of carefully observing how students identify and manage challenges in a text.

How Not to Build a Sofa

On her show *Ellen's Design Challenge*, Ellen DeGeneres challenges six designer/furniture-maker teams with design tasks. On a recent episode, four teams were charged with designing a sofa that fit in an empty space in the lounge on the set. The chairs, coffee table, end tables, and lamps were all in place; an empty spot remained for the winning team to fill with the perfect couch. The teams worked feverishly to create beautiful couches within the forty-eight-hour time limit. In the end, all of the designers were excited about their sofas and confident about their chances to win the design challenge.

And then the judges walked onto the set to evaluate the sofas. The first thing they did was . . . sit on the sofas! This was surprising, because the design teams had given little thought to the comfort of their sofas. One was so big that the judges' feet didn't touch the floor; another was too deep; and another had hard, pointed armrests.

Each of the sofas was lovely in its own right, but the judges declared that there was no winner for that night's challenge. None of the sofas worked with the other furniture in the lounge *and* were comfortable to sit on, thus none of the designers met the original design challenge. While the designers *began* the sofa challenge with the end in mind—designing a comfortable sofa that matched the other furniture in the lounge—they became distracted by fabrics, ornamentation, and design. They didn't hold on to the end goal.

Similarly, when we imagine readers who are independent and proficient, we picture students who integrate a host of reading strategies automatically, work to solve problems when they arise, read for their own purposes, and chase their interests through books. Like the sofa designers who created sofas that looked good but weren't comfortable to sit on, we too often develop readers who know how to practice isolated strategies—question, infer, synthesize, clarify, and so on— but who aren't reading for the deepest meaning of a text or reading for the love of it. Like the designers, we have a design challenge—developing readers' independence and proficiency—and, working backward from it, we must keep the end goal firmly in mind, paying just enough attention to would-be distractors, such as text levels, reading strategies, and graphic organizers, to end up with agentive readers.

What We Hope to Accomplish with This Book

Interests in student agency and reading for the love of it naturally bring up questions about how instructional mainstays such as read-aloud, shared reading, guided reading, and independent reading should look in classrooms where teachers are letting students do more of the work. These instructional contexts have long histories of representing "best practices" in literacy, yet conflicting "do this, don't do this" messages have left teachers questioning what role, if any, each of these instructional contexts should play in their instruction. *Who's Doing the Work?* is rooted in the belief that when we are mindful about allowing students to actively engage their reading processes, each of these instructional contexts contributes richly to children's reading growth and development. In this book, we offer a vision for adjusting these practices to better align with the end goals of independence, proficiency, and joyful reading.

How This Book Is Organized

Because developing a smoothly operating system for integrating print and meaning is at the heart of this book, Chapter 1 explores the reading process and offers educators a model for better visualizing what reading independence and proficiency look like. In Chapters 2 through 5, we look at each of the four instructional contexts—read-aloud, shared reading, guided reading, and independent reading. We provide an overview of each context and use a dance metaphor to help teachers better imagine the recurring cycle of teaching and learning work that they engage in with students.

In our explorations of read-aloud, shared reading, guided reading, and independent reading, we provide a snapshot of how each structure has traditionally been used to support growing readers and then some ideas for adjusting the structure to accommodate the demands of next generation literacy instruction. We continue with an investigation into what makes the instructional context special and important, clarifying exactly what it is and how it supports readers' growth and development. From there, we offer readers a vision for how each structure can look and offer guidelines for planning lessons.

Because next generation reading instruction requires an emphasis on the reading process, in each chapter we offer suggestions for handling the tricky parts of each instructional context. We also address some misconceptions and tell some cautionary tales. Near the end of each chapter, we offer detailed classroom snapshots of each context to help you translate the ideas in the chapter into practice. Finally, each of these four chapters ends with some reminders and a summary of the ideas presented.

Chapter 6, "Putting It All Together," offers suggestions for how to shift the responsibility for learning from the teacher to the students by using text, language, and instructional context. Offering tips about how to manage time, select books, and focus on reading process, this chapter helps teachers see how to optimize the benefits of the gradual release of responsibility using each of the instructional contexts—read-aloud, shared reading, guided reading, and independent reading—to support the end goal—the design challenge—of independence and proficiency.

A Different Story

We wrap up this introduction with a story that serves as a counterpoint to the stories we started with. It offers a picture of the possibilities for student agency as we expect students to do much more of their reading work.

Kim pulls up alongside Celia, a third grader reading Poppy *(Avi 1995). Celia eagerly reads aloud the following passage from this "great book about a brave mouse":*

> Wanting to look away, she glanced at the base of Mr. Ocax's tree. There lay what appeared to be a mound of pebbles. Gradually a ghastly realization came over her. What she was seeing was a mound of Mr. Ocax's upchucked pellets, the closely packed and undigested bits of fur and bone from his dinners. The vision made her blood turn cold. Only the sound of Mr. Ocax's sneering voice jolted her back to alertness. (48–49)

When she arrives at the word "ghastly," Celia glances at Kim. Kim cocks her head and before she can say anything, Celia says, "I know. What am I going to do?" Placing her finger beneath the word, Celia says it slowly and methodically. She mutters, "I have no idea what that means" and begins to think aloud. "Mr. Ocax is the owl that Poppy is always trying to avoid. He's killed other people in Poppy's family. Poppy's scared of Mr. Ocax. I think this word is connected to Mr. Ocax being evil. I think I need to read on to figure it out."

Kim responds, "Yes, I think that could work. You are really taking charge of your reading! I can't wait to hear if reading on helped you."

After the lesson, Kim debriefs with Celia's teacher, Ms. Vernot, who had watched Kim work with Celia and several other students. She exclaims, "I had no idea they could do so much on their own!"

Helping students and the teachers who teach them recognize a reader's power is at the heart of *Who's Doing the Work?* This book is about adjusting familiar instructional practices to let students assume more of the work. It is about moving attention from what the teacher needs to do to what the students should be doing on their own. We have found that repeatedly asking "Who's doing the work?" helps reframe the gradual release of responsibility and has a profound impact on whether or not students grow to become agentive readers.

Chapter 1

Reading Process: Beginning with the End in Mind

Holy Bagumba! A Cautionary Tale

*O*nce upon a time, there was a third-grade girl, Daisy, who loved to read. *She read all the time. While she liked to read about horses and outer space, she especially loved to read stories. She had read every single Magic Tree House, Junie B. Jones, and Amber Brown book ever written. Recently, she had been into reading books about animals and had read* Shiloh *and* Charlotte's Web. *One day, as she browsed through books at the school library, she found a book with a beautiful cover showing a girl wearing glasses holding a comic book. When she saw it, she thought, "That girl looks like me!" She ran her fingers over the letters scrawled grandly across the cover and—after chunking* Ulysses *into parts—read the title aloud:* Flora and Ulysses. *It was then that she noticed a squirrel tucked up in the corner, which made her wonder if the small animal was Flora or Ulysses and compelled her to read the back cover. As her eyes moved over the words describing a story about a squirrel who gets run over by a vacuum cleaner, bizarrely causing him to develop superpowers, she opened the book and began to read. Getting stuck for a few seconds on the word* bagumba, *she managed to figure it out and read on to understand that this was a book she needed to read.*

Before she knew it, Daisy heard the librarian shouting a last call to check out books. She hurried to have her book scanned and joined the rest of the children lined up at the door to return to class. Ms. Wright, her teacher, walked up and down the line surveying the children's choices. Every now and then she'd murmur things like, "Oh! Great author!" and "You'll love this one." By the time Ms. Wright reached her, Daisy was nearly bursting with excitement. She couldn't wait to tell Ms. Wright how she loved what she had read from her book so far. She longed to hear her teacher say what a great choice Daisy had made selecting a book with a medal on the cover.

However, when Ms. Wright glanced at the book in Daisy's hand, she looked at Daisy and said, "Oh, sweetheart, you're going to need to return this book."

Return this book?! Did she hear correctly? *Confused, Daisy looked at her teacher, who kneeled beside her, looked regretfully into her eyes, and said, "You're a level R. This book is much harder than that; it's a level U. Run and give this back. You can choose something from the R bin when we get back to the classroom."*

Crestfallen, Daisy handed the book back to the librarian. In her head, she heard Flora's words—the words she had just worked so hard to figure out: "Holy Bagumba." As she turned to line up empty-handed, she muttered to herself, "What am I going to read now?"

Back in the classroom, Daisy dragged herself to the R bin and, without even looking, grabbed the book that was on top. She returned to her seat and muttered the title: Captain Underpants and the Attack of the Talking Toilets. *Grudgingly, she began to read . . .*

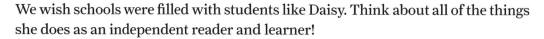

We wish schools were filled with students like Daisy. Think about all of the things she does as an independent reader and learner!

- She chooses to read books that require her to work hard.
- She reads for meaning, even when a book is difficult for her.
- She stops to work on words when she has trouble decoding them.
- She chunks long, unknown words into more manageable parts.
- After figuring out an unknown word, she rereads to make sense.
- She is an avid reader.
- She is selective about what she reads and has particular tastes in books and authors.
- She likes to read books with characters that remind her of herself.
- She knows how to preview the book by looking at the cover and reading a bit.
- She knows that medals on book jackets mean that other people who read the book thought it was very good.
- She is very intentional in her book selection.

- Once she has chosen a book, she gets very excited about it.
- When she is excited about a book, she looks forward to telling her teacher about it.
- She sees herself as a reader.

Daisy's skill, interest, and knowledge of books and of herself as a reader all epitomize our goals for students and could translate into her enjoying an agentive identity as a reader across her lifetime. Daisy's current independence, interest, and willingness to work hard are the end that we have in mind—the end of the gradual release of responsibility, that is—after we have engaged students in read-aloud, shared reading, and guided reading instruction.

However, while Daisy's reading enthusiasm and proficiency are our goal for all readers, too often we see, hear about, and read about work in read-aloud, shared reading, and guided reading that does not mirror the work we see Daisy doing. Rather than teach children to preview texts, we take on the introductions. Rather than teach them to wonder and notice, we ask them text-dependent questions. Rather than allow students to truly choose books for themselves, we retain control, confining them to narrow reading-level parameters and placing excessive demands for book logs and written reflection. We are not saying that we should never introduce a text, ask text-dependent questions, give students guidelines for selecting texts during independent reading, or assign reading logs. We are saying, however, that it seems that in many classrooms these practices have reached an extreme and are increasingly getting in the way of student independence.

Accompanying these instructional choices are subtle and obvious messages to students. Think about what Ms. Wright's reaction to Daisy's book selection communicates to Daisy:

- I think of you as a reader almost exclusively in terms of your reading level.
- I trust reading levels absolutely and generally don't consider the nuances of your reading process, the text, or your motivation to read.
- Although you think you know how to select a book for yourself, you really don't.
- You are not as good at selecting books for yourself as the others standing in line.

- The confidence you have in yourself is misguided.
- Don't get excited about the books you want to read until you check with me.
- I'm in charge of your "independent" reading.

Unfortunately, Daisy's well-meaning teacher is shortsighted and doesn't recognize the beauty in Daisy's independent reading choice. Though she cares about Daisy and does not mean to thwart her sense of agency, Ms. Wright is blinded by levels and Daisy's upward movement through them. Consequently, Ms. Wright's instruction in read-aloud, shared reading, guided reading, and independent reading hinges too much on levels, which, too often, actually stand in the way of learning.

What Do Reading Levels Mean, Anyway?

Levels have become ubiquitous in schools and are almost universally used to describe students' reading achievement. Not only are students directed to select books from lettered bins or Lexile bands, but in many school districts, teachers receive charts that outline where on a text-level continuum children should be reading at quarterly benchmarks throughout each grade. These charts are intended to help teachers know whether children's reading growth is "on track."

So, for example, if it is the end of the school year and Patrick, a first grader, is reading from level J books, his teacher can rest assured that he is exactly where he needs to be. His classmate Kendra, who is exceeding the standard at level L, is also of little concern. Marcos, however, who is finishing the year reading "below grade level" at level H, is a source of great angst for his teachers, his parents, and school administrators.

But what do leveling systems *really* reveal about children as readers? What do we know about how Patrick, Kendra, and Marcos actually interact with text? Reading levels and their accompanying labels can provide *some* information about a student's reading achievement relative to his or her peers, but there is a pervasive sense in education that they communicate something significant about children as readers. We frequently see teachers with large binders full of data and reports on students and their reading levels. Too often, however, when we listen to the same students read independently and talk with them about what they are reading, we find that far too many of them are reading books that don't fit them, despite the binders full of reports.

Knowing that Patrick, Kendra, and Marcos hit a testing ceiling at levels J, L, and G respectively without knowing what each of these readers actually *does* when he or she interacts with text does little to help us know how to support their reading growth and development. Although many systems for determining students' reading levels include opportunities to look closely at how students read—by analyzing patterns of miscues and ratios for self-correction, for example—it remains far too easy to overlook these rich sources of formative data when assessing students. Administrative pressure on teachers, accountability demands, students' familiarity with test materials, marginal assessment resources, and time limitations all contribute to students frequently being placed in levels that do not fit them and where they are likely to plateau, grow frustrated, and lose their sense of agency.

As we have been observing this pervasive pattern of making instructional decisions largely based on levels, we have also noticed a simultaneous and growing countertrend spurred by thinkers and writers—including ourselves—to build student agency, to think deeply about student reading processes, to loosen the grip of leveled-text thinking, and to strengthen the connections among instructional contexts across the gradual release of responsibility. Thought leaders such as Dorothy Barnhouse, Vicki Vinton, Debbie Miller, Regie Routman, Gail Boushey, Joan Moser, Chris Lehman, Stephanie Harvey, Richard Allington, Peter Johnston, Mary Howard, Kathy Collins, Kylene Beers, and even Fountas and Pinnell are calling for less teacher talk, fewer contrived instructional experiences, and more student engagement and empowerment as readers. Fountas and Pinnell explain, "We must go beyond the letter and focus on the process." They further implore us to "change what you're noticing and teaching to support self-monitoring, self-regulating systems" (2015).

In contrast to the narrow thinking that forced Daisy to put down *Flora and Ulysses* (DiCamillo 2013) and pick up *Captain Underpants and the Attack of the Talking Toilets* (Pilkey 1999) or the competitive pressure felt by Patrick, Kendra, and Marcos's teacher, next generation thinking considers *how* students read as much as *where* in the text gradient they read.

Teaching That Focuses on Students' Reading Processes

One of the reasons that the language of levels is so pervasive is that it is compact. Letters, Lexiles, and other reading-level metrics feel objective. They seem to take the complexity of student reading and magically represent it with a single metric. In contrast, reading processes, particularly as they are analyzed in benchmarks and running records, are messy and don't lend themselves to quick discussions in the hallway or with parents. In fact, whole books have been written about various theoretical models of how children read. But somewhere between the single metric of reading levels and entire textbooks on how students process texts, there lies an accessible vocabulary that can enable conversations about reading process without bogging us down in long descriptions of how—and debates about whether—children are using print, meaning, and structure.

An Enabling Vocabulary Around Reading Processes

As she studied children learning to read, Marie Clay identified three sources of information that readers use to construct meaning: (1) the context, including the pictures, (2) the print, and (3) the syntax or language structure (1979, 1991). Building on this work, Burkins and Croft combine meaning with context and syntax and explain in practical terms, "Basically, when one thinks of the pragmatics of reading instruction, there are two 'biggies': Students have to read the words *and* understand them" (2010, 3). In next generation reading instruction across read-aloud, shared reading, small group reading, and independent reading, our conversations about reading level should rest on how students handle these two "biggies." Consider the following questions about how individual students use print and meaning to understand text:

- Do students monitor their accuracy and their comprehension as they read?
- How efficiently do students cross-check and self-correct?
- How deeply do students comprehend?
- What do the students do when they get to words they don't know how to decode?
- What do students do when they get to a word they don't understand?
- How do students navigate the nuances of text features at different levels?

Ultimately, the goal is for readers to smoothly and automatically integrate print and meaning in ways that allow them to appreciate text for both the information it provides and the response it evokes. When we are skilled at observing and understanding students' reading processes, we become better able to support students' reading growth and development through text selection, direct instruction, conferring, and so on.

How Do *We* Read?

To further your understanding of children's reading processes, we have set up a series of three texts that will place specific limitations on *your* reading process. While contrived, these exercises will offer you insight into how reading works.

Efficient Reading

The following passage has a few words missing. As you read it, note what you do to figure out the missing words.

> "I'm H_ _ _ _ _ _ _ Granger, by the way, who are you?"
> She said this all very fast.
> Harry looked at Ron, and was relieved by his stunned face that he
>   hadn't learned all of the course b_ _ _ _ by heart either.
> "I'm Ron Weasley," Ron mut_ _ _ _ _.
> "Harry Potter," said Harry.
> "Are you really?" said H_ _ _ _ _ _ _. (Rowling 1997, 106)

What did you notice about your reading process as you read the passage above? As a proficient reader, you engaged a host of reading strategies. Read the list below and see which descriptions fit the way you approached reading and understanding the text excerpt:

- Looked at the first letter of the missing word, noticing both the letter and whether it is upper or lower case (print strategy)
- Skipped the unknown word to read on and gather information (integrated strategy)
- Eliminated words that don't start with the identified letter (print strategy)
- Looked at the length of the word, as indicated by the number of dashes (print strategy)
- Eliminated words that are too long or too short (print strategy)
- Looked to see if there were other letters available that you knew (print strategy)

- Eliminated words that do not sound right (meaning strategy)
- Read complete sentences to understand the context (meaning strategy)
- Activated background knowledge (meaning strategy)
- Narrowed background knowledge to information related to the Harry Potter books (meaning strategy)
- Thought of words that would make sense *and* begin with the correct letter *and* sound right (integrated strategy)
- Tried possible words out in the blanks and reread to check them (integrated strategy)
- Reread the text to think about any deeper meanings or subtleties you may have missed (integrated strategy)

Notice how many strategies you used for just a couple of sentences! Figuring out the missing words required you to utilize both print *and* meaning and, ultimately, to integrate the two. If you began searching for an "H" word to insert in the first blank, you looked to the meaning to support your efforts to figure out the unknown word. If you began by thinking about a word that would make sense, you checked your hunches against the available print information to make a reasonable guess.

Either way, your flexibility in using the print to support the meaning or vice versa allowed you quickly and easily to figure out the tricky parts and continue reading, which is a hallmark of a smoothly operating, integrated reading process. In terms of representing your reading process, the Venn diagram in Figure 1.1 illustrates your comparable skill with print and meaning. The overlap between the two circles represents your integration of strategies.

Figure 1.1

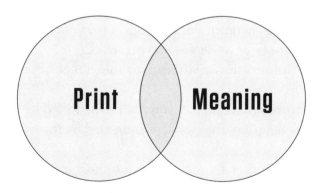

An Efficient Reading Process

When children's reading processes work as yours worked here—in relatively balanced, integrated ways—they make steady, predictable, even self-extending (Clay 1994) progress through increasingly difficult text, and levels become secondary markers to how well they read and how quickly they progress.

Favoring Print

In contrast to the more balanced reading process you practiced above, there are a number of reading habits that readers can develop that, over time, can cause reading progress to plateau or can simply make readers inefficient. To illustrate, we offer you a second text to read. Once again, as you read, pay attention to your reading process. How does it change? Are you still able to integrate print and meaning smoothly?

> Fluid retention and edema have been observed in some patients taking NSAIDS, including CELEBREX. NSAIDs should be used with caution in patients with fluid retention or heart failure. NSAIDs, including CELEBREX, may diminish the antihypertensive effect of angiotensin converting enzyme (ACE) inhibitors and angiotensin II antagonists, and in some patients can reduce the natriuretic effect of furosemide and thiazides. (Pfizer 2015)

Unless you have a degree in medicine in addition to a degree in education, or unless you or someone you love suffers from arthritis and you have studied the related medical terminology, it is likely that the passage above placed very different demands on you than the excerpt from *Harry Potter and the Sorcerer's Stone*. In *When Kids Can't Read: What Teachers Can Do,* Kylene Beers says, "*Anyone* can struggle given the right text. The struggle isn't the issue; the issue is what the reader does when the text gets tough" (2003, 15). So what did *you* do when you read this particular text?

Given the concentration of rather long and, most likely, unfamiliar words—such as *angiotensin, natriuretic,* and *furosemide*—you probably found yourself automatically slowing your rate in the last sentence, chunking the long words into likely syllables, and relying more than usual on the print information in the text. You probably had limited background knowledge on which to draw, although you could quickly categorize this jargon-filled passage as a bit of medical-ese and could figure out that many of the unknown words had to do with some kind of medical condition. Your reading process in this text probably looked something like Figure 1.2, with much attention paid to the print information and considerably less to all of the available contextual information.

Figure 1.2

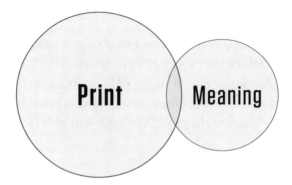

An Inefficient Reading Process:
Overrelying on Print Information

While this simulation is contrived, and your adjustment of your reading process was an efficient way for you to tackle a challenging text, some children exhibit a similar imbalance in all of their encounters with text. When children demonstrate extreme print dependency, they tend to have gaps in their understanding of the text or may not construct meaning at all. They may read every word beautifully, while their comprehension is limited or nonexistent. Children who read superficially, without really thinking about the meaning of a text, also overdepend on print, although the pattern may be less obvious. To understand this, think about what happened when you read the passage about Celebrex. Did you feel like you understood it deeply? If you're like us, probably not. However, see what you notice when you refer to the passage and take the following comprehension test:

1. What is one example of an NSAID?
2. What is one drawback of NSAIDs?
3. What type of enzyme does Celebrex sometimes inhibit?
4. What did you learn about NSAIDs?
5. What do you think is the author's purpose for writing this text?
6. Would you recommend Celebrex to a loved one? Why or why not?

Chances are, you could answer most of these questions. Perhaps your responses to number 4 and number 6 were a little vague, but not without some content. On many assessments, such superficial understanding would be enough to earn you a satisfactory rating for comprehension and allow you to graduate to text at this level, or even move on to an assessment at the next level. Can you imagine, however, if all of your instructional and independent reading was required to be at this level? What do you think would happen to your reading process? Most likely, the same thing that happens to children who regularly employ a print-dependent process for reading would happen to you—you'd continue to work really hard to figure out how to pronounce the words while only gaining a cursory understanding of what they mean. Furthermore, all the practice of an inefficient reading process would likely habituate print overdependency. Eventually, you would probably begin to read all texts this way, even those that you once read efficiently.

Favoring Meaning

While a tendency to overrely on print can explain why some children's reading progress stagnates and why some children lose interest in reading, it is not the only cause of these patterns. To gain insight into another plausible explanation, read the following cloze passage and, once again, notice your reading process— the ways you integrate print and meaning to figure out the unknown words. On a piece of paper with lines numbered 1 to 6, write the words you insert in the blanks as you complete the following:

> We know more about how to engage diverse people in processes of deep 1 _____ that generate ownership and establish conditions for continuous improvement. What makes this revolution real, not 2 _____, is that changes in technology and pedagogy are also becoming dramatically 3 _____. Essentially, the case in *Stratosphere* is that the trio of technology, pedagogy, and change 4 _____ makes for an unbeatable combination. The convergence is so 5 _____ that we may well see in the immediate future multiple lines of breakthrough solutions radicalizing how we 6 _____. (Fullan 2013, 5)

With no letters to assist you in figuring out the words in the blanks, your only choice as a reader is to insert words that would make sense based on the information provided immediately before and after they appear, as well as to pull in information synthesized from considering the larger context of the passage. While your guesses may *feel* reasonable, without any print information, it is impossible to know for certain whether the words you slotted in were the words the author intended. This guessing without cross-checking can create the sometimes false impression that you understand better or more than you think. In the following paragraph, the words in italics indicate the guesses we generated when we tried this exercise:

> We know more about how to engage diverse people in processes of deep 1 *reflections* that generate ownership and establish conditions for continuous improvement. What makes this revolution real, not 2 *contrived*, is that changes in technology and pedagogy are also becoming dramatically 3 *important*. Essentially, the case in *Stratosphere* is that the trio of technology, pedagogy, and change 4 *potential* makes for an unbeatable combination. The convergence is so 5 *compelling* that we may well see in the immediate future multiple lines of breakthrough solutions radicalizing how we 6 *teach*. (Fullan 2013, 5)

To further illustrate our point, look at Table 1.1 and compare the meanings of our guesses with the meanings of the words that actually belong in the blanks.

Table 1.1

Guesses and Answers for Cloze Exercise

OUR GUESS	ACTUAL WORD
1. reflections	1. improvement
2. contrived	2. hypothetical
3. important	3. compelling
4. potential	4. knowledge
5. compelling	5. strong
6. teach	6. learn

As you can see, in some cases, such as with number 3, where we said "import-ant" and the actual word was "compelling," our guess reasonably approximated and preserved the message intended by the author. However in most cases, the words we chose substantially compromised the meaning of the text. Figure 1.3 represents students' reading processes when they pay much attention to the con-textual information and insufficient attention to the print information.

Figure 1.3

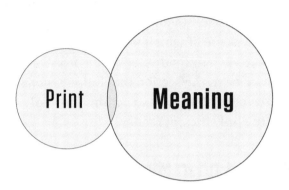

An Inefficient Reading Process:
Overrelying on Meaning Information

The simulation above, of course, is contrived in that there are no circumstances that we can think of when students would not be able to use print to cross-check their approximations. The Venn diagrams, however, *do* illustrate very real hab-its that many children develop when learning to read. Readers who develop too much dependency on meaning information will often overlook some or all of the print in a text and guess based on what they understand about the story. While relying on meaning in this way is a sound strategy to employ occasionally, these readers habituate their neglect of print cues. When these readers encounter text about topics with which they are unfamiliar, reading suddenly becomes very dif-ficult, and, once again, progress is likely to stagnate.

A Word About Generalizations

With experts continuing to debate which parts of the reading process are most important, reducing reading processes to a set of Venn diagrams may feel like an oversimplification of reading's complexities. The Venn diagrams in this chapter, however, can offer insight into whether students have a tendency to rely on one system over another. They can also help us plan instruction that supports children in developing reading processes that integrate print and meaning in relatively balanced and efficient ways as they grow to be eager and self-motivated—just like the student we introduced earlier, Daisy.

Most educators who write or talk about how reading happens describe the integration of information that takes place during reading as "the" reading process. We understand, however, that reading processes are idiosyncratic; they are more like fingerprints than one-size-fits-all gloves. While there are general patterns for interacting with text, some of which we have explored in the previous pages, there are also nuances to each individual reader's process that should inform our instruction. As we describe in the section that follows, consideration of these nuances will help you develop literacy instruction that truly supports children as they become thoughtful and efficient readers.

Beginning with the End in Mind

To grow and develop as readers, children need instruction that mirrors the "end" goal—readers with smoothly operating, balanced reading processes who feel empowered and motivated to take charge of their reading lives. Knowing a student's reading level, however, does not tell us anything about *how* that student reads, so reading-level designations and benchmarks are insufficient as end goals for our instruction.

Let's think again about Patrick, Kendra, and Marcos, who we met earlier in this chapter. They are all at the end of their first grade year, and Patrick reads at level J, Kendra at level L, and Marcos at level H. At first glance, it seems quite obvious that Kendra is the best reader in the bunch and that Marcos is at risk, but looking at their reading processes paints a more complete picture of them as readers.

Patrick's Reading Process

Though Patrick is technically reading "on grade level," his reading process, represented in Figure 1.4, is inefficient. It involves excessively guessing based on context and then rereading and self-correcting when his original substitution does not make sense. Patrick self-corrects most of his miscues, but not because his reading process is efficient. Rather, he has mostly read texts with very familiar content, which have allowed him to rely too much on meaning. Lately, his teacher has been teaching his guided reading group from informational texts on unfamiliar topics, however, and Patrick's wobbly reading process is showing up prominently. Despite his grade-level designation, Patrick is very shaky when he can't count on his background knowledge, and his teacher is quite concerned.

Figure 1.4

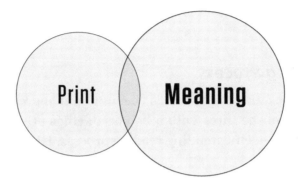

Patrick's Reading Process

Kendra's Reading Process

Kendra, who looks and sounds like the best reader among the three, actually has issues with comprehension. She understands texts superficially, much the way you probably understood the medical disclaimer for Celebrex that you read earlier in this chapter. Kendra's reading process is illustrated in Figure 1.5.

Figure 1.5

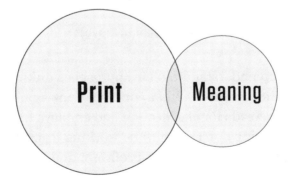

Kendra's Reading Process

Kendra's talk about text lacks depth. With her ascent through text levels, Kendra's lack of attention to meaning (and her reliance on print) has become more troublesome. Among the three readers—Patrick, Kendra, and Marcos—Kendra is actually the reader with the most compromised reading process and the one the teacher should be most concerned about. She needs very specific support in learning to think deeply about what she is reading, and this will take strategic instruction. Like Patrick, Kendra is stuck, even though she is one of the "highest" readers in the class.

Marcos's Reading Process

By contrast, Marcos, our student who is "behind" and of greatest concern, is actually the only one of the three with a balanced, efficient, smoothly operating, and—most important—self-extending reading process. His reading process is illustrated in Figure 1.6.

Figure 1.6

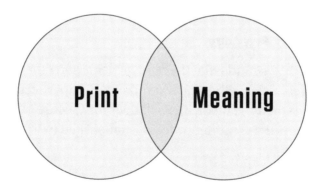

Marcos's Reading Process

Marcos reads for deep understanding. He approaches unknown words with intention and automatically checks his approximations against his background knowledge. He even rereads for clarification and employs fix-up strategies when the print and the meaning don't seem to be working together. Summer reading holds great promise for Marcos, who is proficient and balanced at level H and who is highly motivated and agentive as a reader. If Marcos has access to great books at increasingly difficult levels, he will be able to grow his reading process over the summer and return to school in the fall ready to join Patrick's guided reading group. Marcos—with his below-grade-level designation—is actually the *best* reader among the three!

Fortunately, when instruction emphasizes reading process throughout read-aloud, shared reading, and guided reading, we end up with more readers with a reading process like Marcos's and fewer readers who overrely on one cueing system. Each instructional context, from read-aloud through independent reading, makes a unique contribution to students' growth in proficiency and agency. Teaching across the gradual release of responsibility with an emphasis on reading process—versus an emphasis on reading level—will change the way you teach reading forever.

Closing Thoughts

In the beloved story *The Alphabet Tree*, Leo Lionni (1968) describes the heart of the reading process. Initially the letters, who are characters in the book, are concerned only with how they go together, with making individual words, and with understanding their connections to one another. Pleased with themselves, the words rest on individual leaves until a caterpillar crawls into the scene. "Why don't you get together and make sentences—and mean something?" he asks (22). So the letters assemble themselves to form sentences: "The bug is small" and "Leaves are green" (24). The caterpillar pronounces their efforts good, but not good enough. "Why?" the letters ask in surprise. "Because you must say something important," responds the caterpillar (26–27). The letters think and plan, then craft a message of peace and deliver it to the President.

So the big ideas of learning to read, which are those of figuring out the code and those of thinking deeply, are presented by Lionni with a few letters, some leaves, and a caterpillar. We have read extensively about various models of "the" reading process, and although these inform our work, we must say that we like Lionni's model best. Basically, readers have to understand how letters work and how to think deeply to construct meaning. The point, after all, is to understand something important.

Questions for Reflection

1. In what ways have reading levels served or not served you as a teacher?
2. In what ways did the experience of reading the series of three sample

texts give you insight into how reading works?

3. In what ways did this chapter push or shift your thinking?

4. Think of a specific child you teach. Draw a Venn diagram that approximates a representation of his or her reading process.

5. What questions did this chapter raise for you? What questions did it answer?

6. With what in this chapter did you agree? With what did you disagree?

Chapter 2

Read-Aloud: Giving Students a Reason to Learn to Read

*O*h, *that story! I never, never could have thought of anything so beautiful. When it was over—I couldn't help myself—I forgot to raise my hand, and I cried out, "Oh, please, teacher, read it over, read it over!"*

Then I was aghast because I had called out and I thought Miss Lang would punish me. But she gave me a lovely smile and said, "When you learn to read, you will be able to read that story all by yourself."

I became a scholar that day. I hung on Miss Lang's words and did whatever she told me to do. Miss Lang said that learning the letters was the beginning of reading. So when I lay in bed at night, I stroked my ABCs on my pillowcase and made consonant sounds under my breath. I learned to read—quickly, quickly.

—Laura Amy Schlitz

Of the many structures used to support children on their journey to become readers, read-aloud is quite possibly the one most celebrated by children. From the warm feelings evoked by coming together with peers to thinking about and discussing a compelling story to the delight of hearing the cadence of beautiful words, read-aloud can be rapturously engaging and serve children in both obvious and not-so-obvious ways—not the least of which is by planting the desire to learn to read, as was the case with Joan, the narrator in the excerpt above.

What Is Read-Aloud?

Read-aloud is a teaching structure that introduces students to the joy of constructing meaning from text. During read-aloud, teachers are the only ones with access to the printed text, and they assume all of the responsibility for negotiating the print, thus freeing students to focus their attention on the meaning. Together, teachers and students explore aspects of the text such as relevance, personal connections, themes, author's purpose, word choice, the interplay of words, text structure, and especially the ways a powerful text can change us. The collective background knowledge and emotional reactions of the group, combined with explorations of textual elements, allow teachers and students to mine text for subtle meanings that are not obvious at first. When students find a text difficult to understand, teachers can help them resolve confusion by posing questions such as "Which part does not make sense to you?" and "What could we do to figure that out?" Teachers may also think aloud, modeling the oftentimes messy process of piecing together bits of information to reach a deep understanding of text.

As is the case with each of the other instructional contexts across the gradual release of responsibility—shared reading, guided reading, and independent reading—text selection is paramount for an effective read-aloud. Generally, the text for read-aloud is significantly above grade level, meaning that most students would find it very difficult, or even too difficult, to read the text on their own. However, *difficult* should not be synonymous with *boring* or *ridiculously hard*. When selecting text for read-aloud, it is important to search for topics, authors, and genres that students find very engaging. Read-aloud is a commercial for learning to read. It entices children to lean into the tricky parts of a text for the reward of enjoying its meaning, and this understanding of the relationship between productive effort and its joyful benefits can motivate students during shared reading, guided reading, and independent reading.

Dancing Lessons as a Metaphor for Understanding Read-Aloud

In this chapter and the next three chapters, we present learning a dance as a metaphor for the recurring process of learning about how reading works and working in increasingly difficult texts. An aspiring dancer watches a graceful and proficient dancer glide across a dance floor and becomes completely immersed in the experience *for its own sake*. The dancer-to-be watches a skilled dancer who is so graceful and elegant—and appears to be having such a wonderful time—that he or she says, "I want to do that."

Similar to the narrator in the excerpt from *The Hired Girl* that opens this chapter, the reader or reader-to-be—who acts as a listener and a thinker during read-aloud—has the opportunity to become immersed in the experience and enjoy read-aloud for its own sake. The read-aloud provides a context as the child becomes absorbed in the text and the power of the meaning-making experience and says, "I want to do that."

Developing dancers, however, watch proficient dancers for different purposes. In addition to watching for joy and inspiration, they watch to gain insight into *how* the skilled dancer dances so beautifully. The dancer in training may watch his or her teacher demonstrate a new dance all the way through at the beginning of the cyclical process of learning a dance, or he or she may watch a YouTube video of a favorite dancer in order to acquire new moves. The student watches with intention, and the teacher may share insight into the process to support the dancer's development.

Just as watching a new dance serves a dancer in different ways, read-aloud serves multiple purposes for readers. In terms of the gradual release of responsibility, read-aloud represents the way a student experiences the joy of a dance while simultaneously nurturing the skill needed to be able to do it alone. Students first watch and become involved with a dance (constructing meaning from text), then later explore it alongside the teacher (shared reading), then practice under the watchful eye of the teacher (guided reading), and finally dance (or read) independently. As the developing dancer becomes proficient in one dance, the process begins again, and the dancer's skill continues to grow through inspiration and practice.

The Evolution of Read-Aloud

Throughout the various phases of standards-based instruction, read-aloud has been ostracized to some degree. The diminishment—and even complete loss—of read-aloud in classrooms drains energy from reading work and contributes to factory-style education, where only educational investments with obvious, immediate test-score payoffs warrant instructional time. Recognizing that read-aloud is a long-term investment in students' growth and development—as humans, as members of a community, and as readers—teachers are increasingly reclaiming its important role.

Conventional Read-Aloud

During conventional read-aloud, the teacher may summarize the text in the introduction or preview vocabulary. The teacher reads the text, usually stopping frequently to ask questions or provide prompts that usually have a specific answer. If there are illustrations, the teacher shows them to the entire class, particularly if working with young students.

Teachers commonly select read-aloud texts for their relationship to particular instructional standards or because the texts introduce, reinforce, or illuminate certain reading strategies for students. They may also think aloud during the reading, modeling the ways they approach the various demands of the text.

Next Generation Read-Aloud

Next generation read-aloud, like conventional read-aloud, involves the teacher reading out loud from a single copy of a text. Teachers may still, on occasion, select texts that lend themselves to teaching particular instructional standards. In next generation read-aloud, however, there is much less teacher talk. Teachers may even (imagine this!) read-aloud a text for its own sake, engaging students in conversations about the text's meaning and enjoyable parts of the text, *without* explicitly capitalizing on standards-based teaching points, which tend to interfere with student engagement. Next generation read-aloud presumes that reading aloud to explore the benefits of productive effort with text and to discuss the ways a text makes us think are just as standards based as reading aloud to explicitly teach specific learning targets. Table 2.1 highlights key differences between conventional and next generation instructional practices in read-aloud.

Table 2.1

Comparison of Conventional and Next Generation Read-Aloud

	CONVENTIONAL READ-ALOUD	NEXT GENERATION READ-ALOUD
VALUE	Read-aloud is often considered less valuable than other instructional contexts, which may lend themselves better to explicit instruction.	Read-aloud is considered invaluable as a motivational tool and as a way to demonstrate a meaning-making process.

	CONVENTIONAL READ-ALOUD	NEXT GENERATION READ-ALOUD
PURPOSE	Read-aloud is used to explicitly teach instructional standards or discrete reading strategies.	Read-aloud is used to make students eager to learn to read, to help them understand themselves and each other, and to *sometimes* explicitly teach standards or discrete reading strategies.
TEXT SELECTION	Texts are selected mainly for the discrete standards or reading strategies they can introduce, reinforce, or illuminate for students.	Text selection is based first on the anticipated level of engagement of the students—particularly around sophisticated ideas—and second on the teaching opportunities the text provides.
TEACHING POINT	The teacher explicitly instructs through much of the read-aloud; there is extensive teacher talk, direct instruction, and explicit connections to instructional standard(s).	The teacher reads aloud the text to engage students and facilitates or prompts discussion for collaborative construction of meaning. The teacher *may* make limited, intentional teaching points based on particular instructional standard(s).
READING WORK	The teacher carries all of the print work and also heavily supports students' comprehension, often guiding (or driving) conversation in a predetermined direction.	The teacher carries all of the print work but leaves to students most, if not all, of the work of teasing out and constructing the meaning of the text.
DISCUSSION	Discussion is based largely on teacher-prompted questions, which are often text based and/or close ended.	Discussion is based largely on what students notice or wonder about the text.

Why Is Read-Aloud Important?

In the gradual release of responsibility model (Pearson and Gallagher 1983), read-aloud offers readers a demonstration of proficient reading. It shows them what engagement with a text—problem solving and thinking deeply—"looks" like.

Basically, through modeling, read-aloud teaches the *how* of interacting with a text and the *why* of meaning making from texts.

A vast ocean of research supports read-aloud—particularly with accompanying discussions—as an instructional tool across grade levels. While it is beyond the scope of this book to dig into the "plethora of empirical research about the benefits" of reading aloud (Layne 2015, 6), we do want to mention some of the commonly appreciated (and documented) advantages for readers. Read-aloud increases receptive and expressive vocabulary, improves fluency, strengthens comprehension, and increases motivation to read, to name a few. Furthermore, the more students are read aloud to, the more these benefits tend to increase (Walsh 2008).

What Makes Read-Aloud Special?

Ask a group of adults to describe their favorite memories of school, and they are likely to describe times when a teacher read aloud to them. Whether remembering how they laughed out loud when Wilbur tied a string to his tail and jumped off the manure pile to make a web in *Charlotte's Web* (White 1952) or how they gasped when Violet Beauregarde turned into a giant blueberry in *Charlie and the Chocolate Factory* (Dahl 1964) or how they wept at the end of *Where the Red Fern Grows* (Rawls 1961), the powerful emotion of read-aloud experiences anchors them in our memories. While this power has much value in its own right, it brings with it a host of additional benefits, some of which we describe here:

> *Read-aloud allows all students to focus on the meaning of the text.*
>
> Learning from excellent texts is highly engaging in any instructional context, but read-aloud is an equal-opportunity instructional strategy because the barrier of the text is eliminated. Consequently, discussions during read-aloud focus on collaboratively constructing meaning from the text. This productive effort tends to be less stressful than in reading experiences where students must work through the print before they can access the meaning. Rich discussions and relaxed engagement with compelling texts make read-aloud joyful and give those who have difficulty with print a chance to engage with their peers around texts that would otherwise be inaccessible.

Read-aloud develops social imagination.

Reading allows people to vicariously participate in experiences. Because reading aloud gives children access to sophisticated characters and plots, they begin to better imagine and understand what life can be like for others, which helps them better relate to other people. It teaches empathy by lending voice to others who may have very different experiences and opinions. This social imagination also serves students by showing them the consequences of actions without the students actually having to live the experience. By learning about characters and events in the context of group discussions, students broaden their perspectives.

Read-aloud builds community.

Read-aloud experiences involve "performances" of beautiful texts, intermingled with stimulating discussions that often affect the way the participants see themselves, others, or the world. These powerful shared experiences connect members of a group in lasting ways, helping them understand each other better and giving them reference points for connecting with each other in the world beyond the read-aloud.

Read-aloud gives students a reason to work hard to become better readers.

Read-aloud is a potent reminder of the power of text. Students who demonstrate limited interest in reading or who have difficulty with reading come to understand the value of becoming readers as they watch, listen, discuss, and learn the benefits of productive effort. Read-aloud is a commercial for reading.

Read-aloud gives students a safe space to explore complicated topics.

Read-aloud provides a safe, supported context for discussing difficult topics, such as bullying, racism, or death. Such discussions provide teachers opportunities to learn about students' opinions and feelings while giving students space to process big ideas. Read-aloud events that explore complex ideas can help students understand each other and themselves and give them a point of reference for understanding what it means to live together as humans.

Read-aloud gives students access to texts that would otherwise be too difficult.

Because it involves texts that are beyond students' independent and instructional levels, read-aloud exposes students to ways of thinking, to ideas, and to vocabulary that stretch them. Explorations of sophisticated texts prime individual experiences with increasingly difficult text, paving the way for reading growth.

What Is the Work of Next Generation Read-Aloud, and Who Is Doing It?

Because of its place at the beginning of the gradual release of responsibility and because only teachers can see the text, it is natural to assume that teachers do most of the work during read-aloud. It is true that the responsibility of negotiating print belongs exclusively to teachers, but the responsibility for making meaning is shared by teachers and students. Learning to enjoy the ways language communicates beauty, ideas, information, and story is critical for motivating students to want to read better and more on their own. Sometimes teachers have to provide models for how to notice and talk about these aspects of text; actively involving students in this work provides them opportunities to practice the skills needed to enjoy a text both aesthetically and efferently (Rosenblatt 2004). This supports their ability to make meaning as they work across the gradual release in shared, guided, and independent reading. As much as possible during read-aloud, the work of constructing meaning should be done by students.

What Should Next Generation Read-Aloud Look Like?

Read-aloud lessons share particular commonalities. The following list, while not exhaustive, shares many of the basic and important elements to consider as you shift your thinking to next generation read-aloud practices:

- The teacher is in front of a group of students with a book in hand.
- The students are seated comfortably—often on the floor—to optimize their enjoyment of the read-aloud experience.
- The teacher reads aloud the text to the students in highly engaging or animated ways.

- The students listen with rapt attention. Responses may range from rapt silence to uproarious laughter to audible gasps.
- The teacher stops periodically to allow students to discuss their responses to and observations about the meaning of the text.
- The teacher's reading and support of student discussions makes obvious that he or she has carefully explored the text prior to sharing it with students.
- The text prompts enthusiastic responses and engaged discussion from the students.
- The teacher prompts students to think about *how* they deepen their understanding of the text and what they wonder, connecting their productive effort to their reading processes.
- If the book includes illustrations, the teacher shows them to the students when reading the related portion.

How to Implement Next Generation Read-Aloud

Just as there are many types of read-aloud—from a picture book read in a single sitting to a chapter book read over several days—there are many ways to plan for and implement read-aloud, one of which we describe in this section. As with all instructional contexts, careful planning helps to optimize teaching opportunities and enhance the learning potential offered during the read-aloud.

Prepare

Preparing for a successful read-aloud includes carefully selecting the text and planning potential stopping points to engage students in brief discussion. The paragraphs that follow describe this process in more detail.

Select the Text

Text selection is the first, and potentially the most important, aspect of planning a successful read-aloud experience.

Consider the interests of your students. Select a text that they are sure to find engaging *and* that gives them substantive ideas to discuss. Although texts that are funny or gross, texts that originate in pop culture, and mass-produced texts are often "engaging" for students, text choices should also be *excellent*. Try looking for these qualities when searching for texts that are engaging *and* high quality:

- texts that offer insight into the experiences of children their age but who live very different lives
- texts that introduce students to fascinating topics or information
- texts that offer new perspectives on familiar topics or ideas
- texts about topics students have said they want to know more about
- texts by familiar or beloved authors

Consider the reading levels and the speaking vocabulary levels of your students. Generally, the read-aloud text is one that most students in the class could not read on their own. The ideas in the text should give students much to talk about and should leave them talking even after the read-aloud experience is over.

Consider the text relative to the other texts you have read aloud to students. Ask yourself: How much racial, socioeconomic, gender, and age diversity is presented in the texts I share with students?

Consider factors such as genre and opportunities for addressing vocabulary, skills, and strategies. Remember that great texts have the inherent power to teach in spite of us, but if the texts *aren't* engaging, teaching opportunities will be limited.

Preselect Stopping Points

Conversation is critical to optimizing the learning value of read-aloud. Thinking in advance about where you will stop to engage students in discussion has the potential to lead to richer conversations and deeper insights. Here are planning steps that we find helpful:

1. Read the text thoroughly.
2. Identify the purpose of the read-aloud, which could include modeling a comprehension strategy, teaching a particular standard, practicing thinking about a text, or engaging students in a joyful experience with a book.
3. Jot down open-ended questions that *may* facilitate conversation throughout the read-aloud. You will use these, as needed, to support conversation and to further student discussion. Consider asking questions like these:

   - What are you thinking about?
   - What are you wondering?
   - What ideas do you have?
   - What are you noticing about ___?

- How does this make you feel? Why?
- What does this make you wonder?

4. Anticipate where students might experience difficulty seeing subtleties or understanding meaning woven into the text. Mark these places with a sticky note.
5. Develop text-based questions to use *if* students need additional support or direction during the read-aloud.
6. Depending on the difficulty or complexity of the text, consider practicing reading it aloud to ensure a smooth presentation.

Present

Invite students to get comfortable before you begin reading aloud. Depending on your preferences and the classroom culture, this may mean inviting students to assemble in a meeting area in the room.

Read

Begin reading aloud. If you are reading a picture book or article or just beginning a chapter book, spend a little time introducing the text. Look at the front cover together, talk about the author, and allow students time to make spontaneous predictions and set their own purpose(s) for reading.

Pause

Invite students to turn and share their thinking with a partner or a small group at either your preplanned stopping points or when interests, questions, or difficulties arise. Remember that read-aloud is an active process and the more opportunities students have to talk, the more engaging it is.

Listen In

As students discuss their responses to open-ended questions or practice thinking in the ways that you model, move through the group to listen to their conversations and take anecdotal notes.

Share

After students have had the opportunity to discuss their ideas with partners or small groups, you may choose to invite them to share with the whole group. It is not necessary to process and share after every turn-and-talk. In the interest of keeping the read-aloud engaging, limit whole-group conversations to discussing only the most important points that come up during student discussions.

What's Tricky About Read-Aloud?

By and large, read-aloud is a relatively straightforward instructional context; however, the process of supporting students as they construct meaning together is filled with complexities. To heighten your awareness of pitfalls, assist you as you plan, and help you optimize the benefits of read-aloud, we offer the following sections describing challenges that commonly arise and suggestions for addressing them.

Finding Texts That Are Culturally Relevant

Finding excellent texts that represent diversity—racial diversity, socioeconomic diversity, diversity of beliefs, gender diversity, and so on—can be difficult. Inequities in representations of people in publications persist, but more and more strong texts are becoming available that have main characters from underrepresented groups. It is important for students to experience texts with characters who are like them as well as texts with representations of people who initially appear unlike them. Persist in your efforts to expose students to all kinds of diversity, working with colleagues to identify overlooked biases in your text selection. Periodically, examine the body of texts you have read with students to pinpoint perspectives you want to include more.

Preserving the Beauty of the Experience

Although few people debate the value of read-aloud, especially when texts are selected for the reading skills and strategies they can teach students, some have trouble seeing the value of reading aloud for its own sake. For this reason, read-alouds can lean in the direction of overly instructional, resulting in learning experiences where the story is lost in a sea of too much teacher talk. Experiencing the way words come together to form ideas and noticing how words, ideas, and stories affect us as human beings is at least as important as pointing out text features and explicitly showing students how to infer using clues provided by the author. Pay attention to how much time it takes to get through relatively short chunks of text. Also note the balance between teacher talk and student talk. If it is taking a long time to get through relatively little text *and* you are doing most of the talking, chances are the value of the read-aloud is being compromised.

Keeping the Discussion Focused

Because children are largely inexperienced with formal discussions, they will sometimes want to use the read-aloud conversation as a platform to talk about tangential topics that don't necessarily contribute to deepening understandings of the text. Young children in particular tend to want to talk about everything that springs to mind, so it can be especially challenging to help them think deeply about the book without squelching their enthusiasm as they talk about what happened to their dog last night or why they don't like eggs. When conversations go astray, making statements such as "Let's get back to the book" or asking questions such as "How does that idea help you understand the text better?" can help reclaim the conversation.

Involving Everyone in the Discussion

It is common for a handful of students to respond quickly to the text or discussion prompts whereas other students need more time to process or tend to be more quiet. While interactive read-alouds tend to encourage spontaneous contributions to conversations, you will have to counterbalance the spontaneity with the important role that each person's voice plays in a community. Experiment with letting students turn and talk with each other before responding, or ask students to sit and think (and wait) for about thirty seconds so that everyone has a chance to formulate ideas. Varying seating arrangements can also help balance voices.

Letting Students Do the Work of Meaning Making

Teachers, with their agendas for using a text to support children's reading growth and development, can have a tendency to overdirect and monopolize conversations. In read-aloud, talk plays a critical role in helping children learn to mine text for its nuances and subtleties. It is important that students have plenty of opportunity to practice processing their ideas about text and to make their productive effort public. Likewise, pausing to ask yourself "How much am I talking?" can help you reflect on the appropriateness of your role during discussion and help you pull back if necessary.

Deciding How to Use a Text to Support Students' Ability to Make Meaning

Because read-aloud begins with great texts, teachers are naturally faced with a multitude of teaching opportunities, making it difficult to decide which opportunities to seize. Seizing them all may feel like a solution to this problem, but using a single read-aloud session to present multiple teaching points can rob a book of its teaching potential altogether. Such attempts inundate children with information that they can't process in the time they are given. We find it is better to select one salient point to serve as an instructional focus for a read-aloud. Also, remember that not every read-aloud has to have an explicit teaching point, and that the implicit learning in a read-aloud is just as valuable and standards based. Plus, great books can always be read again!

Making Sure Our Selections Represent Many Different Types of Texts

Read-aloud has traditionally favored narrative texts, and though inadvertent, our affinity for story oftentimes leads us to select more fiction than nonfiction. It is important to remember that read-aloud offers students exposure to rich vocabulary, builds background knowledge about text structure and content, and allows children opportunities to formulate insight and ideas. When text selection favors one type of text over another, we limit the type of vocabulary, background knowledge, and ideas that students have access to, which can stymie students' progress in other instructional contexts. Keep a running list of titles you read aloud to students and periodically review it through the lens of text type, making sure that your read-alouds offer enough variety.

Giving Read-Aloud the Time and Attention It Needs

Teaching schedules are often crunched by all sorts of unexpected demands and interferences, leaving teachers to make decisions about what to keep and what to cut. Oftentimes, because of its reputation for being "that fun thing we do after lunch," read-aloud gets cut first. We urge you to resist this tendency, because the benefits of read-aloud are critical to student reading growth and development. It is an instructional context that gives students supported opportunities to explore *how* to make sense of text through productive effort, allowing them to take new insights, strategies, energy, and purpose into shared reading, guided reading, and independent reading. If you have to make cuts to instructional contexts, do so evenly, so that one aspect of your instruction—read-aloud, for example—does not bear the brunt of reduced instructional time.

Misconceptions About Read-Aloud

We find that one of the most common misconceptions about read-aloud is that its only value is that it is "fun." Stop and think of your three strongest positive memories from school—more than likely, at least one of them involves a teacher reading aloud to the class. While the inherent joy that is common in read-aloud experiences seals these events in our memories, read-aloud's value extends much farther than pleasure. In fact, the research on the benefits of read-aloud is so strong that the lack of attention to the context in classrooms is puzzling. Steven Layne rightly asks, "If we all want to be 'research based' (and it seems to me that these days nearly everyone does), then why don't we listen to such a significant and consistent body of evidence?" (2015, 10).

It seems that, somewhere along the way, some educators began to become suspicious of the inherent pleasure and joy that comes with reading aloud to children and developed the notion that if it's that fun, then perhaps read-aloud is not instructionally sound. Unfortunately, this notion has led to some schools issuing directives to limit—or even forbid—read-aloud in classrooms, which is particularly distressing to us. Part of the problem is the misconception that participating in a read-aloud is a passive, rather than an active, process. Because students do not interact with the print directly, the uninformed wrongly assume that participating in read-aloud is of limited value.

Directives to limit or forbid read-aloud may also be rooted in the common belief that while appropriate for young children, read-aloud is of little value to older students. Planning for read-aloud is a thoughtful, intentional process that involves carefully selecting texts for a particular audience. When teachers are mindful of factors such as length and complexity, all types of texts—picture books, chapter books, articles, and information books—have the power to stretch and grow readers.

Cautionary Tales and Nonexamples of Read-Aloud

Even though read-aloud seems like an obviously simple instructional context, it is actually pretty sophisticated and nuanced. Because it is misunderstood, there are a number of common ways that the instructional agenda can actually rob read-aloud of its amazing power, some of which we describe in the sections that follow.

Facilitating "Open-Ended" Discussions with a Veiled Agenda

Students can lose interest and energy in even the most engaging books if the discussion doesn't provide them an opportunity to share their ideas openly. Having a hidden, specific, comprehension agenda—*What is the main idea of this passage?*—or asking questions that feel open-ended-ish but for which you are really seeking a specific response, will cause children to quickly grow weary of the guessing game. If you find yourself responding to student answers to your questions—answers that are correct but not what you were thinking of—by saying things like, "Yes, but I was thinking of something more _____. Does anyone else have any ideas?" then you are probably doing too much of the work, robbing students of learning opportunities, muting student agency, and draining the read-aloud of energy. Stop!

"Read-Aloud" with Students Actually Reading the Text

The basic premise of read-aloud, whether conventional or next generation, is that the teacher reads the words of the text out loud. Students do not read or even see the text during a read-aloud. Round-robin reading or any variation where individual students read portions of the text aloud are not read-aloud.

Teaching the Book to Death

With the advent of standards-based instruction, it has become common to presume that the purpose of read-aloud is to explicitly teach standards or reading strategies. Although this is sometimes valuable, when supplemental teacher talk takes over the read-aloud time, the teaching actually kills the read-aloud experience. There is still room for explicit instruction in next generation read-aloud, but there should be regular read-aloud experiences for the sake of enjoying and exploring an excellent text, with instruction that is a natural outgrowth of authentic conversation.

Listening to a Recording of the Text Without Any Discussion

There are many wonderful recordings of books now available, many of which involve stellar performances by celebrated readers. We feel that although listening to a recording eliminates some of the magic and intimacy of the experience, a powerful recording of a story can introduce other kinds of magic and engage students in different ways. In both cases—listening to the teacher read and listening to an audiobook—the critical element of the read-aloud experience is the discussion! In fact, the text is simply a conduit for ideas—a pathway to thinking, connecting, and learning. If you play audiobooks without stopping to ask students what they notice, think, and wonder, you aren't really facilitating a read-aloud, next generation or otherwise.

Read-Aloud with Mediocre Books

You will discover—if you haven't already—that a recurring theme in this book is that text selection is the most important element of a strong reading experience. This point cannot be overstated in regard to any of the instructional contexts, and read-aloud is no exception! There are too many excellent books out there and there is no excuse for wasting a minute of instructional time with books that are marginally appealing, have no substantial ideas, or present uninspired illustrations.

Books That Are Way Too Hard

Read-aloud should usually involve books that are substantially beyond the average reading level of the group, but this does not mean that they should be so hard that the teacher has to elaborate or offer an explanation every few sentences. If students are unable to grasp the meaning of the text without extensive work from you, the book is probably too hard, even for read-aloud.

Classroom Snapshots: Next Generation Read-Aloud in Action

The following snapshots present three different read-aloud sessions, each in a different grade level. As you read these, imagine yourself reading aloud as students listen intently. Pay careful attention to the "work" of this instructional context: What does the teacher do, and what do the students do?

First Grade

Knowing that the first-grade class she will be working with will soon start a science unit about animals, Jan thumbs through her collection of nonfiction books. She is looking for a book with an assortment of text features and something that will hold the students' interest. She decides on *Rainforest Animals* by Michael Chinery (1992), because it seems to strike the right balance between animals that students will recognize and be excited to see in a book—like chimpanzees and tigers—and animals that likely will be unfamiliar—like tarsiers and kinkajous.

On the day that Jan visits the first graders, the students gather on the carpet and many notice that she is holding a book "with a bird on the front." She hears Lorena say that she saw that bird when she went to the zoo. The students settle in next to their reading partners, and Jan turns to the first page and carefully holds it open so that the children can see the illustrations. As she moves it slowly from right to left so that the students seated on the floor can get a good look at the picture, she says, "Turn and talk to your partner about what you notice about this page."

As the student pairs chat, Jan notes that none of them talk about the "Do you know?" box in the lower left corner or other text features, such as the "Rainfor-est Facts" in the top middle of the page and the map of the world marked with yellow to show where rainforests are located. Instead, she hears conversations about the big blue butterfly—"That thing is huge!"—and wonderings about the little animal with big eyes hiding on the branch near the bottom of the tree. After the students finish their conversations, she reads the text beneath the heading "Life in the Rainforests" that ends with "Animals live at all levels in the forest, from the ground to the treetops" (4). After reading that sentence she says, "I know that many of you are wondering about some of these animals, especially this one right here." Jan points to the creature with big eyes that she heard so many of them discussing. "Give me a thumbs-up if you would like to know more about this animal."

All of the children hold up their thumbs and nod eagerly. Jan continues, "This book has lots of bits of information written all over the page, which means that we don't have to start at the beginning and read to the bottom of each page in order. We can skip around! Because you want to know more about this animal, let's see if we can find it in our book."

Jan turns the pages slowly. When the students think they've identified the an-imal, they begin to point and shout that they see it. Jan looks at the picture and flips back to the first page so that students can compare. They decide that while the nocturnal aye-aye looks similar, its eyes are much smaller than the animal on the first page. Jan turns to the next page where the children see the big-eyed tar-sier. Certain they have identified the creature correctly this time, they ask Jan to read about it. They want to know, "What does it say?"

As she begins to read the first sentence, "Tarsiers are little relatives of mon-keys" (11), Connor begins to wave his hand wildly. When Jan tries to continue to read without calling on him, he blurts out, "I saw monkeys when I went to the zoo with my grandma!" The students spontaneously begin to share monkey stories and Jan, interested in following their lead without getting pulled too far out of the book, says, "Hmm, you are doing what readers do! You are thinking about what you already know about monkeys. You obviously know a lot about monkeys already. Let's take a minute and tell our partners what we already know." After giving students a couple of minutes to share their monkey stories with each other, Jan asks a few students to share with the whole group. Students are in agreement that monkeys "eat bananas." Jan says, "Let's continue to read to find out even more about monkeys, especially this one. I wonder if it eats bananas."

The students settle again to listen to the description of the big-eyed tarsier and, when Jan finishes, they turn to talk about what they found interesting. Many are astonished that tarsiers eat small animals, because they were so certain that all monkeys ate "bananas and leaves and stuff like that." One of the students points to another monkey on the page and asks, "Does it say what that one eats?" Driven by their need to know what monkeys eat, Jan reads about the chubby colobus monkey and then flips through the pages looking for other apelike creatures. When she finds one, she reads aloud the information about that animal to help the children learn more about monkey diets.

Third Grade

As she prepares for a read-aloud with a group of third graders, Kim sifts through the texts sitting on her shelf, pulls a few favorites, and begins to reread, carefully noticing the words and illustrations. Thinking about the rich conversation that another group of third graders recently had about how people grow and change over time, Kim decides to use William Joyce's *The Fantastic Flying Books of Mr. Morris Lessmore* (2012).

After lunch, Kim joins the third graders as they gather in the meeting area in the back corner of the room and listen as she opens the book and begins to read. She has planned that she will pause for a little discussion after she reads the page that says the following:

> Then a happy bit of happenstance came his way. Rather than looking down, as had become his habit, Morris Lessmore looked up. Drifting through the sky above him, Morris saw a lovely lady. She was being pulled by a festive squadron of books. (12)

Kim stops and says, "I bet you have noticed a few things. Turn and talk to the person next to you about what's on your mind."

Chatter about the book begins promptly, and Kim grabs a clipboard and weaves through the students seated on the floor. She leans in to listen as Maria and Patrick talk about how "dark" the pages were and then how "on this page with the balloons it became colorful." She jots down their insight and waits to see if they say more. Their conversation stalls and Kim says, "What an interesting observation! Why do you think the book does that?"

Dominic, who is talking to Leslie, explains that in the first part of the story, "Morris Lessmore was writing his story and it got all blown around so maybe he was sad and that's why it was, like, all gray. I think he's a lot happier on this page."

Kim continues to listen as a few other pairs of students talk and she hears that many of them have noticed the same color change that Maria and Patrick had noticed. She returns to her seat, places the book in her lap, and starts turning the pages so the students can have a second look at the illustrations. As they look at the pages again, Kim says, "What ideas do you have about these pictures?"

Immediately, hands shoot up across the classroom and students talk about how they see three different types of colors in these pages—orangeish, grayish, and bright. They conclude that the illustrations are really important in this book because they tell how Morris Lessmore is feeling. They decide to watch the colors in the illustrations more closely as Kim continues to read the story.

Later that week, long after discussions about Mr. Morris Lessmore have concluded, Mr. Jenkins, the classroom teacher, contacts Kim to tell her about Jillian, a student in his class, who returned one afternoon from recess visibly upset. He relays that when he asked her what was bothering her, she explained that she had had a fight with one of her friends, which made her feel "just like the beginning of the Mr. Lessmore book. All the color is gone."

Fourth Grade

On the Monday after Thanksgiving break, Mr. Arnold picks up the book he'd been reading aloud to his class before their holiday, Kate DiCamillo's *Flora and Ulysses* (2013), and perches on the stool in the front of the classroom. He waits as his students shift into comfortable positions in their chairs. Before he begins to read aloud Chapter 11, "A Gigantic Vat of Incandesto," Mr. Arnold says, "It's been a few days since we've visited Flora. Take a minute before we start and talk to your neighbor about what's going on in the story so far. Specifically, try to remember what happened last."

As the students converse, Mr. Arnold walks around listening to what students talk about. He notices that they are animated as they recall Mrs. Tickham vacuuming up Ulysses and notes that Tory, when recounting the part about Flora smuggling the distressed squirrel into her bedroom, tells Michael her own story about smuggling a baby turtle into her house after finding it at the community pool. Satisfied that his students both remembered and understood what was happening, he turns to page 32 and begins to read, "She put Ulysses down on her bed, and he looked even smaller there in the bright overhead light."

He continues reading until the bottom of page 35:

> "Incandesto!" she said. "See? Alfred T. Slipper becomes a righteous pillar of light so painfully bright that the most heinous villain trembles before him and confesses!"
>
> Flora realized that she was shouting the tiniest bit.
>
> She looked down at Ulysses. His eyes were enormous in his small face.

When he reaches this point, Mr. Arnold stops and says, "Talk to your partner about what you are thinking."

Mr. Arnold notes that students are chatting quietly and listens carefully as his students talk about their thoughts. He realizes that most of them are summarizing what they understand—that Flora is explaining to Ulysses that after he was sucked up by the vacuum cleaner and after being rescued, he had awakened with superpowers. When he listens in to Saul and Tyreque, however, he hears something else:

"I don't get what Mr. Slipper has to do with it. Who is this 'Incandesto' that she keeps talking about?" asks Tyreque.

"I know. And what the heck was she even saying at the end? I didn't get that at all," Saul replied.

Mr. Arnold leans in and says, "I wonder if other kids might be wondering the same thing. Would you mind sharing what you just said to each other with the whole class?"

After listening respectfully to Saul and Tyreque's questions, the students begin to clear up the confusion by reminding them of how they already know that Flora is into reading a comic with "a really fancy name." As they talk, they begin to describe Flora: "She is like really smart or something." Mr. Arnold probes the students to say more about that. They talk about how Flora calls herself a "cynic," and they ask Mr. Arnold to read that last part over again:

> "Incandesto!" she said. "See? Alfred T. Slipper becomes a righteous pillar of light so painfully bright that the most heinous villain trembles before him and confesses!"

The students begin talking, saying things like "who really talks like that?" and "I don't even get what half those words mean," and "See? That's how you know she's really smart!"

Excited to have figured out something important about Flora, the students beg Mr. Arnold to continue reading. However, before he does, he says, "Wow, I can see how you are growing as readers! Think about what you just did. You recognized when you were confused, you knew that in order to clear up the confusion you'd have to reread, and you didn't go on until you were certain you understood. I remember when the school year began, many of you didn't even notice when things didn't make sense!" Responding to further student pleas, Mr. Arnold perches himself on his stool, opens up the book, and continues.

Read-Aloud Reminders

- Make it your mission to find excellent, highly engaging texts that communicate substantive ideas and give students a lot to think about. The book is everything.
- Give students opportunities to construct meaning and create knowledge through productive effort.
- Prompt students' reflections by helping them understand their reading processes and the strategies they will use to figure out text in less supported instructional contexts.
- Make read-aloud joyful, through both excellent text choices and generous opportunities to enjoy the benefits of lively, productive effort.
- Focus first on exploring the text. Explicit instruction is a secondary purpose for reading aloud.
- Keep teacher talk to a minimum.
- Remember to read across genres: poetry, biography, informational texts, newspaper articles, and more!
- It is okay (fabulous!) to read aloud for its own sake. It will make children

want to read, and children who want to learn are easier to teach and more successful.

- As much as possible, let student responses and inquiries guide the discussion about the text.
- Let books open the door for students to think and talk about big ideas, such as social justice and how they want to change the world.
- Reread as often as possible, especially those books that just beg to be reread.
- Repurpose read-aloud texts by using them in shared reading and guided reading—depending on the reading levels of students—and by making them available for independent reading.
- Remember, the student role during a read-aloud should be active, not passive.

Next Generation Read-Aloud: Chapter Summary

Like the dance performance that makes us long to dance ourselves, read-aloud shows students why they are working so hard to learn to read well. Next generation read-aloud focuses on read-aloud's powers of engagement while still leaving room for intentional but limited teacher talk. It follows the lead of students as much as possible, making space for responsive teaching, reflective connections to standards or isolated strategies, and celebrations of productive effort. Because read-aloud is the first step in the gradual release of responsibility and because the print work is carried exclusively by the teacher, read-aloud offers magical opportunities for students to practice creating knowledge together—knowledge about texts, which can help them become better readers, and knowledge about life, which can help them become kind humans. As Joan expresses in the quote that opens this chapter, read-aloud helps children learn to read more quickly.

Read-Aloud Ideas to Try

- Listen carefully to what children are talking about during the discussion about a text. Pay attention to the quality of the conversation and the depth of the thinking and use these formative data to adjust instruction during read-aloud and shared reading.

- Reread a text several times to students and note the way the discussion evolves with each reading.
- Fall in love with a book and then read it to your class without making any explicit teaching points! Let the book do the teaching, as all excellent books do.
- Video record yourself during your read-aloud. When you review the video, note how much work kids are doing to make meaning relative to the volume of teacher talk. How can you increase the former while decreasing the latter?
- Video record a read-aloud and review the children's affective responses to the text. Are they literally leaning in? What evidence is there of student engagement with the text?
- Video record a read-aloud experience and review which students are participating in the discussion. Are some students saying little or nothing? Are some dominating the conversation? Explore and implement strategies and seating configurations that help quiet students feel safe enough to speak up and vocal students learn to listen. Record another read-aloud and see how student patterns of contributing to the discussion have changed.
- Document when students select read-aloud books for independent reading. What percentage of the books you read aloud do students later read independently? What conclusions might you draw from any patterns you notice? Meet with colleagues to discuss ways to further explore the connection between books read aloud and books students select to read on their own.
- During read-aloud, have students sit as if they are on a bus, leaving an aisle so that you can move easily amongst them and listen in as they discuss their ideas about the text.

For Further Reading About Read-Aloud

Story: Still the Heart of Literacy Learning by Katie Cunningham (Stenhouse 2015)

In Defense of Read-Aloud: Sustaining Best Practice by Steven Layne (Stenhouse 2015)

The Read-Aloud Handbook by Jim Trelease (Penguin 2013)

Chapter 3

Shared Reading: Bridging the Gap Between Read-Aloud and Guided Reading

*W*hen children get the idea that written words can tell them something absolutely horrible, half the battle of teaching reading is won.

*And that's when I turn to the Titanic. The children sit on the rug at my feet, and
I tell them the story. It's almost scary to have the absolute attention of that many
young minds.*

*I bought a little cardboard model of the ship and spent a week and a half folding
down flaps and inserting tabs to assemble it.*

*I used up three years' worth of bonus points from the Lucky Book Club to buy a
classroom set of Robert Ballard's book* Exploring the Titanic: How the Greatest
Ship Ever Lost Was Found. *It's written on a fourth-grade reading level—lots of
hard words—so I tipped in pages with the story rewritten on an easier level. But by
the end of the second week the children are clawing up my pages to get at the original
text underneath.*

—Bailey White

Like read-aloud, shared reading offers delightful opportunities for building
a reading community and for teaching children to think about how reading
works. Shared reading combines the auditory engagement factors of the teacher reading aloud, the visual engagement factors of following along in the text,
the emotional pull of an excellent text, and the cognitive lure of productive effort. Shared reading presents one of the richest and most inviting opportunities
to offer students guided practice in increasingly difficult texts. During shared

reading, as in the preceding story, students are eager to read texts that would be beyond them otherwise.

What Is Shared Reading?

Shared reading is an instructional structure designed to support students as they read texts that would otherwise be too difficult for them to access independently. Developed by New Zealand educator Don Holdaway (1979, 1980), shared reading offers students opportunities to collaborate with the teacher to solve some of the problems presented by text. The collaboration was originally designed to emulate the fun and interactive nature of lap reading, where parents and children explore the print and the meaning of a text together.

The hallmarks of shared reading are the shared text—everyone can see the print—and the unison reading, usually with the support of a lead reader. Students engage in a variety of problem-solving opportunities, depending on the challenge presented by the text (Parkes 2000). Older students may simply follow along as the text is read aloud by a teacher (Allen 2002), occasionally stopping to discuss the meaning, explore vocabulary, or analyze the structure of a word. Students may use bookmarks to indicate their place in the text, which allows the teacher to monitor their silent reading to some degree. During these shared reading experiences, teachers—with students—make notes about how print works and how meaning is constructed, often creating anchor charts for reference during guided or independent reading.

In other shared reading experiences, students are invited to read the words aloud with the teacher. Teachers stop to discuss print- or meaning-related tricky spots—either spontaneously discovered during the reading or preselected by the teacher. This back-and-forth holds students accountable for problem solving, allowing them to do the work. The whole-class involvement provides everyone a model for figuring out solutions to various reading dilemmas. The teacher may cover up a challenging word and ask students to draw from past experiences to integrate print and meaning, in order to decode and figure out the meaning of the word. This helps to build children's repertoire of strategies for solving the problems that occur when reading.

While there are many variations on shared reading—buddy reading, reading along with a recording of a text, dualog reading, and so on—this chapter focuses on emerging trends in implementing shared reading. This focus does *not* imply, however, that other practices are no longer relevant or worthwhile!

Dancing Lessons as a Metaphor for Shared Reading

Once again, we turn to the dance metaphor, focusing on the part of the lesson when our imaginary dance class practices the new dance with the instructor. Having carefully selected a choreography that is at the edge of the students' ability but that is not so difficult that the attention of the group will wane due to frustration, and having demonstrated the dance to the students (read-aloud), the teacher begins leading the students in whole-class practice of the dance. During this group practice, the teacher faces the mirror in front of the students and moves through the steps at less than full tempo. Students follow along, matching their steps to the teacher's.

Because students are just learning and because the dance is on the leading edge of the students' skill—in other words, it is a new dance and relatively challenging—most students will miss some (or even many) steps, often at different points in the dance. The teacher's movements remain constant, however, serving as a reliable scaffold for the students as they work out the dance *for themselves*. If several students have difficulty at the same spot, the teacher will work with the whole class to help those students who have stumbled explore the challenges and nuances of the tricky part. Thus, all the students gain insight—either from the teacher or from their own inquiry—into the portion that was tricky for some.

Similarly, in next generation shared reading, the teacher's voice provides the meter and the movement that students must follow, just as Bailey White does for her first graders in the opening quote of this chapter. In shared reading, students must do the reading themselves, whether aloud (the predominant mode in lower elementary) or in their heads (the predominant mode in upper elementary). Like the dance teacher, the reading teacher doesn't stop during the reading if individual children stumble at various points in the text. Such stumbling is expected, as the text is difficult for most of the students in the room. Rather, the teacher holds the pace of the reading steady so that students can find their place and jump back in. At particularly tricky places, the teacher will support the students in thinking about their reading process as they figure out how to solve the dilemma the text presents. This dilemma may be a decoding challenge presented by the print or a comprehension challenge presented as students work to understand the text.

Shared Reading Then and Now

Although originally created to replicate lap reading experiences with young children (Holdaway 1979, 1980), shared reading's versatility has made it a valuable instructional context across grades. The following is a general description of original applications of shared reading as compared to the broader, more contemporary evolution explored throughout the remainder of this chapter.

Conventional Shared Reading

During shared reading, teachers of young children present students with an enlarged text—usually a Big Book—which they read together, often in a singsong manner following the voice lead of the teacher. The level of the text may be slightly or significantly above the average reading level of the class, and teachers may use sticky notes to mask words.

Next Generation Shared Reading

Teachers in any grade, but particularly in elementary school, present students with a shared text, either by passing out printed copies, displaying the text on a screen, or presenting students with an enlarged version of the text, such as a Big Book. Students read along—either aloud or in their heads—as the teacher reads the text aloud at a steady, slightly slowed pace. The teacher stops at strategic points to engage students in conversations as they work through the tricky parts of the text, reflect on their integrated use of strategies, and even makes notes about how they figured out the text's challenges. The teacher intentionally connects shared reading to read-aloud and guided reading, and supports students in transferring the processes practiced in shared reading to their guided and independent reading. Table 3.1 highlights the ways shared reading has evolved.

Table 3.1

Comparison of Conventional and Next Generation Shared Reading

	CONVENTIONAL SHARED READING	NEXT GENERATION SHARED READING
AGE OF STUDENTS	Students are primary age.	Students are all ages.
TEXT ACCESS	The text is usually a Big Book on an easel or a poem transcribed onto chart paper.	Students access text in multiple ways, including Big Books, poems on charts, printed copies, text displayed on a screen, or individual copies of books or articles.
TEXT LEVEL	The text is slightly or significantly above the average reading level of class.	The text is slightly or significantly above the average reading level of class.
TEXT TYPE	The text usually has a pattern, rhyme, or singsong quality	The text may have a pattern, rhyme, or singsong quality; it may also be a single chapter from a book, a magazine article, website content, and so on.
LESSON DESCRIPTION	Students read text together in a singsong manner following the voice lead of the teacher. The teacher may stop to discuss or explore particular print or meaning features of the text.	The teacher stops at strategic points to engage students in strategy conversations. Teacher and students collaborate to discuss and work through the tricky parts of the text, reflecting on their integrated use of strategies and even making notes about how they solved the reading's challenges. Students may read aloud with the teacher or read silently to themselves as the teacher reads aloud.

Why Is Shared Reading Important?

In the gradual release of responsibility (Pearson and Gallagher 1983), shared reading serves as a bridge between read-aloud and guided reading. When children, particularly those who are not reading at grade level, receive little to no shared reading practice, moving up to the next reading level is often too big a leap for them to make because they have no exposure to the texts they are growing into next. This can cause guided reading groups to plateau as students get stuck in a level.

Shared reading presents children with text that falls somewhere between the difficulty levels of read-aloud and guided reading. Shared reading primes students with upcoming vocabulary and text features while also helping them formulate visions of their reading futures. In the end, this work in hard-but-not-too-hard text saves instructional time, as students who regularly participate in shared reading tend to progress through the text gradient more quickly. This is particularly true when, during subsequent guided reading sessions, students have access to anchor charts from shared reading lessons and are encouraged to draw on their shared reading experiences as they problem solve.

What Makes Shared Reading Special?

The benefits of shared reading are often overlooked, perhaps because it is relatively simple to implement (people may presume that its ease of use implies limited benefits) or because it is traditionally used with prereaders and early readers. We think, however, that it may be the most powerful arrow in your literacy quiver. Here are some of the things we love about shared reading:

Shared reading is spectacularly engaging!

We can think of few things that we do in classrooms that are as joyful as shared reading. Something about exploring a great text together—problem solving, discussing, laughing—is intrinsically fun. It could make one wonder if shared reading is "real" instruction, but of course it is.

Shared reading encourages a growth mindset.

We often underestimate the thrill of cognitively challenging work. However, because shared reading involves sharing the work of figuring out the tricky parts of a text, students continually feel the gratification that comes from saying "Yes!" or "I got it!" Not only does this fortify the connection between effort and success, it also teaches children to press on when they face reading challenges during guided reading and independent reading.

Shared reading can serve as a vehicle for exploring content.

Because any interestingly complex text is fair game for shared reading, the structure provides an excellent opportunity to weave content related to social studies, science, or math into language arts instruction. This opportunity to consolidate curriculum has dual benefits. In addition to learning how to process and think deeply about the new ideas presented in a content-specific text, students learn and practice important skills and strategies for reading informational text.

Shared reading helps children progress faster in guided reading.

When shared reading work is intentionally connected to guided reading, as is the case with next generation shared reading, students make faster progress through guided reading levels and groups are less likely to plateau. It is our experience that students who participate in shared reading two or three times a week—even if it means they participate *less* in guided reading—make more progress than students who have guided reading every day with little or no intentionally connected shared reading. This means shared reading is a huge time saver.

Shared reading offers an efficient way to realign out-of-whack reading processes in students.

When students read difficult texts, teachers can expect students' reading form (reading process) to be compromised (Burkins and Yaris 2014). In intentional ways shared reading distributes the work of solving the difficulties presented by the text in intentional ways, so students receive the support they need to right themselves when their process falters. This collaboration allows them to experience what a smoothly operating system feels like, even in a more challenging text. This type of scaffolding—as opposed to scaffolding that involves heavily preteaching the text—lets students do most of the work.

Shared reading builds the classroom community.

Shared reading's impact on a classroom community is at least as important as its value for reading instruction. When whole groups of children come together around the same text, they share the emotional experience of the text. In addition, problem solving with the people you work with most closely creates a supportive work environment, which in turn contributes to a growing spirit of community in the classroom and makes it safe to take learning risks.

Shared reading offers lots of learning "bang for your buck."

The support students receive in shared reading authentically teaches (in the context of real reading) them strategies that make more challenging text accessible in the other instructional contexts, where students assume more of the problem-solving responsibility. Shared reading texts not only can be repurposed in guided or independent reading but also can provide children continued practice in stabilizing their reading process.

Shared reading builds fluency.

Shared reading offers the benefit of a fluent model. Furthermore, fluency requires a well-integrated reading process, which is the backbone of shared reading. During shared reading, students work together with a teacher to solve the problems that would otherwise impede smooth, accurate reading. With shared reading, children usually get to reread, and frequent rereadings help them experience what a smoothly integrated reading process feels and sounds like.

What Is the Work of Next Generation Shared Reading, and Who Is Doing It?

The work in shared reading is engaging a complete reading process (integrating print and meaning) within connected text. The teacher and the students engage in this work simultaneously. Because the teacher is the more proficient reader and is reading aloud, his or her reading catches students if they stumble. As students self-monitor, matching their voice (whether in the head or aloud) to the text and to the voice of the teacher is also part of the work of shared reading.

Finally, solving together any problems that the text presents—such as decoding complicated words or clarifying comprehension confusion—is the particular work of next generation shared reading. These substantive problem-solving opportunities—sometimes spontaneous and sometimes preplanned—allow students to reflect on their reading processes, identify reading strategies in progress, and develop a growth mindset about reading.

What Should Next Generation Shared Reading Look Like?

As a complement to the more general description of next generation shared reading in the preceding section, we offer a few specifics to help you develop a vision for expanding shared reading instruction in your classroom.

- As the teacher reads the text aloud, the whole class reads along—either in unison (usually in primary grades) or silently (usually with older students).
- Students are very excited and engaged.
- There are few, if any, student misbehaviors.
- The class engages in much process-oriented conversation as students figure out the text.
- Students do a lot of reading.
- Teachers minimally explain or tell students how to solve difficulties in the reading. Most teacher talk revolves around supporting students in figuring out the text themselves and in helping them label the strategies they use.
- Reading strategy discussion is in context and often documented on an anchor chart that students will refer to later, during guided and independent reading.

How to Implement Next Generation Shared Reading

As in the read-aloud chapter, this section offers you a way to plan for and implement shared reading in your classroom. When preparing, it is important to remember that shared reading is a versatile instructional context, so the suggestions that follow should be modified to best suit your students' needs.

Prepare

As with read-aloud, preparing for a successful shared reading experience begins with carefully selecting a text. Becoming very familiar with the text you select prior to sharing it with students will help you anticipate possible challenges and make decisions about what skills and strategies you will explicitly address during the lesson.

Select the Text

Select a text that is a level or two above the guided reading level of most of your students, but is still considerably below the level of difficulty you'd select for read-aloud.

Select a text that offers interesting print or meaning work for your students. There should be something in the words, the vocabulary, or the meaning of the text that students can figure out together. Read the text very carefully and make sure that your students will find it engaging.

Figure out how to give all students access to the text during the lesson. You might locate multiple hard copies of the text or plan to display it using a document camera.

Identify Teaching Points

Read the text again, identifying potential teaching points in the lesson. You may cover up or encrypt words to ensure that all students, even those who will read the text with relative ease, have something to figure out and opportunities to reflect on their reading process (Burkins and Yaris 2014). Shared reading is highly useful for demonstrating and practicing cross-checking and self-monitoring, so plan carefully to cover or encrypt the words that lend themselves to exploring the ways the print and the meaning support each other.

Plan Lesson Logistics

Decide how you will present the text and where students will sit during the lesson. This is particularly important because in order for it to be a shared reading lesson, everyone must be able to see the print and illustrations well.

Present

Verify that everyone can see the text. Depending on the level of the text and the purpose of your lesson, you may give students a few minutes to explore the text independently. By definition, most students will find the text difficult, or at *frustration level*. Encourage them to figure out what they can.

Read

Read the text aloud as students read along either aloud (most common in primary grades) or in their heads (most common in upper elementary and middle school). Keep a steady, clear pace that is slightly slower than usual. Read with inflection and energy, modeling how to interpret punctuation and where to put emphasis.

Pause

Stop to let students discuss the print or the meaning at the places you predecided offered important problem-solving opportunities. Ask open-ended prompts, such as "What do you notice?" or "What can you try?" Use specific prompts, such as "Get your mouth ready" or "Read on," as a last resort.

Model and Think Aloud

If you are focusing the lesson on the use of a specific strategy, think aloud as you model the strategy. Keep in mind, however, that modeling specific strategies should not be the predominant practice in next generation shared reading, as it takes too much of the problem-solving work from the students.

Share

Regardless of grade level, shared reading should engage students in a discussion about the text. As much as possible, use think-pair-share to give all students opportunities to think deeply about what they are discovering in the text.

What's Tricky About Shared Reading?

While shared reading lessons are relatively easy to plan and implement, they still present a few challenges. The following sections describe some of the things we find tricky about teaching a shared reading lesson.

Text Accessibility

Everyone in the class needs to see the text in order to read it together, which can be a bit challenging. From rounding up multiple copies of a text to locating a document camera to project texts, addressing text accessibility will take some planning.

Locating Excellent Texts

This dilemma is related to the first one, but we felt it important enough to justify the redundancy. Because shared reading requires everyone to access the text, it can limit the text selection. You must resist the urge to limit your text selection to the six chapter books available in class sets in your book room. Get creative. Having a wonderful text is of primary importance in a next generation shared reading lesson, because the lure of the text entices students to engage in productive effort.

Giving Students Time to Think

It can be difficult to wait for students to figure out portions of the text, which is important for next generation shared reading. Learning the choreography of providing just enough wait time, of teaching children to be patient with each other, and of knowing when to go ahead and just tell students what to do can be challenging.

Balancing Direct and Indirect Instruction

Because of its place at the beginning of the gradual release of responsibility, shared reading provides the ideal opportunity to teach students explicitly how to negotiate the challenges a text presents, how to enlist specific comprehension strategies, how to utilize text features, and so on. That said, it is still ideal for students to do as much of the work as possible. It can be a tricky dance to figure out where to be explicit and where to give students space to explore—even to make mistakes. Basically, if you always explicitly tell students how reading works, or if you *never* tell students what to do, you are probably erring too far toward an extreme.

Connecting Shared Reading to Read-Aloud and Guided Reading

Shared reading's contribution to student reading progress is maximized when you intentionally connect it to read-aloud and guided reading. This, of course, takes very thoughtful planning. Anchor charts that evolve across days offer students ongoing support as they reflect on their reading processes and provide a connecting thread across instructional contexts.

Monitoring Student Participation

It can be challenging to make sure that all students are actually engaged in reading and not passively stumbling through. Because some stumbling is expected as students match their reading to the teacher's—either aloud or in their heads—the challenge is learning to identify the difference between students who aren't engaged at all and students who are engaged but temporarily off track as they figure out how to regain their footing. Learning this distinction comes with practicing shared reading and watching students closely.

Misconceptions About Shared Reading

Shared reading is often portrayed with the image of kindergartners gathered at the feet of their teacher as he or she points to the text in a Big Book. This image has promoted the idea that shared reading is only a primary-grade strategy, causing many educators to dismiss its importance for older students. It is critical to understand that, by design, shared reading allows students to experience reading more difficult text in a supportive, meaningful context. Because shared reading addresses a critical instructional step in the gradual release of responsibility, it is not only a suitable context for children of all ages, but also, we would argue, an essential one.

Another common misconception is that—because students are reading in unison along with the teacher's leading voice—students don't really read, but rather teachers read *for* them. In fact, the work of shared reading is matching the voice of the teacher to the text, which embodies the very heart of the reading process and requires students to *really* read and actively self-monitor.

Cautionary Tales and Nonexamples of Shared Reading

As is common with instructional strategies, the heart of the lesson can sometimes get lost in translation. Here are a few common misinterpretations of shared reading that we encounter in our work with schools.

"Shared Reading" That Is Actually Independent Reading

If everyone has a copy of the text, but they each read at their own pace and then discuss the text as a whole group, it is not shared reading. Lessons that begin with something like "Read this chapter/passage/poem silently and then we'll discuss it" are not shared reading lessons. If students can read the text independently, it is not difficult enough to serve as a shared reading experience. Shared reading texts of appropriate difficulty necessitate "corporate" reading experiences (Holdaway 1979).

"Shared Reading" That Is Actually Round-Robin Reading

If all students have a copy of the text and each student gets a turn to read aloud a sentence or passage to the class, this is not shared reading. While such "round-robin" practices meet the text accessibility requirements of shared reading, they do not meet the engagement requirements. This style of reading "together" is mostly passive and creates behavior management issues, which is the antithesis of shared reading. Furthermore, students are generally less skilled than teachers at providing the leading voice required to smoothly scaffold the class. Please, don't torture your students with round-robin reading.

"Shared Reading" Where the Teacher Talks Through Most of the Lesson

If the teacher talks through much or almost all of the lesson, offering minimal time for students to actually engage in reading the text, it is not shared reading. Beware of mini-lessons that become maxi-lessons, "shared reading" lessons that are mostly about identifying parts of speech in a passage, or lessons with texts that are so difficult that most of the lesson is spent explaining things to students (in the name of "scaffolding"), all of which detract from the authentic reading work that is the heart of shared reading. Remember, the work of shared reading needs to look as much as possible like the reading work students need to practice in order to read independently.

"Shared Reading" with Content-Area Textbooks

While shared reading from a science or social studies textbook may be an efficient way to help students learn the content and therefore *is* legitimate shared reading, it isn't always *sufficient* for reading instruction, because the emphasis likely is on understanding the content-area topic rather than on exploring the reading process. The latter is essential to next generation shared reading. Furthermore, such corporate reading from textbooks is typically less engaging than shared reading with more appealing texts, and solely using content-area textbooks can make your students hate shared reading!

Classroom Snapshots: Next Generation Shared Reading in Action

The following sections present three different shared reading lessons, each in a different grade level. These examples illustrate the reading and thinking work that can happen in shared reading and show the variety of texts and applications. Notice the process-oriented conversations that are central to each lesson. Also, note the way the teacher both guides and follows, giving students abundant opportunities to think, explore, and problem solve.

All three of the lessons illustrate the ways teachers can follow the lead of students while still guiding the lesson in a particular direction. In this book we spend more time describing such implicit, dialogical instruction than describing direct instruction—which usually involves preteaching vocabulary, teaching specific comprehension strategies, or asking preplanned comprehension questions—simply because the latter is more common in classrooms and there are already a number of texts available for supporting it.

First Grade

For a next generation shared reading lesson with a group of first-grade students in early fall, Jan selects Aesop's *The Fox and the Stork* as retold by Mairi Mackinnon (2007). This beginning reader has one short sentence per page, illustrations that support the text, and a story that requires the reader to think—all essential for a strong shared reading lesson. She places the book beneath the document camera so the students can see both the pictures and the words displayed at the front of the class.

On each page, Jan first gives the children an extended opportunity to study the picture and share what they notice or wonder. She does this because this particular group seems to overlook the pictures during guided reading, rushing through the print and missing subtle meaning in the text. She wants to give her students whole-group practice at solidifying a process of studying the pictures before looking at the words.

After students study and discuss the illustrations on each page, Jan moves on to work with the print. She reads aloud the text as the children read along with her as much as they can. On most pages, Jan has covered up one word in the sentence that the students could figure out by looking at the illustrations. For example, on the page that reads "The stork was hungry," the illustration shows the stork sniffing scents coming from the fox's kitchen. On this page, Jan has covered up the word *hungry*. During shared reading, most of the students guess the word correctly, using the illustration as support. Conversations about meaning confirm that *hungry* makes sense.

Before revealing the first letter of the word, however, Jan asks, "If this word is *hungry*, what letters will we see first?" She asks the children to show her a thumbs-up if they think they know the letter, and then she waits until most of the children indicate that they have an answer. When she asks them to say the name of the letter aloud together, most of the children say *h*. Then, Jan reveals the letter *h* at the beginning of the word and the children cheer, certain that the word is *hungry*.

Then, much to her students' surprise, Jan pushes them to think about their reading processes by asking, "How do you know the word is not *happy*?" They pause to think. Vanessa says, "It could be *happy* because both start with *h*, but *happy* doesn't work as good with the story and the picture." Roderick further explains, "If it was *happy*, the stork would be smiling. Look at the stork. It's not smiling." Other students nod in agreement, as Jan reveals the word. "It's *hungry*," they say, with a collective self-congratulatory air.

Once again, Jan does not confirm that their response is correct, but pushes them to look closely at the print. She asks, "How do you know the word is *hungry*?

It starts with an *h* and ends with a *y; happy* starts with an *h* and ends with a *y.*"
After pausing to consider the question, the students articulate the differences in
the middle of *happy* and *hungry* and remind Jan of their earlier references to the
misalignment between the word *happy* and the illustration.

Eventually, Jan confirms that the word is, in fact, *hungry*, and asks students to
reread the entire sentence. This time, she does not read along with them. After-
ward, she summarizes—in the form of congratulation—the work students did.
Jan explicitly reminds them that they used many clues to figure out the word: the
picture, the story, and all the parts of the word. She points out that they made sure
that the print and the pictures matched, and reminds them that any time they figure out a word with one clue, they need to check it with another.

Jan repeats this process of giving the children time to look at the pictures, reading aloud together the uncovered words in the sentence, working through and
confirming the masked words, and reflecting on the problem-solving process
they used. The entire process only takes a few minutes per page. After about 20
minutes, the children show signs that their attention is waning. Committed to
stopping the lesson while students are still enjoying it, Jan reads the rest of the
very short story aloud and lets the children talk about the moral.

Third Grade

It is early October, and Kim brings the book *Biblioburro: A True Story from Colombia* by Jeannette Winter (2010) into a third-grade classroom for a next generation
shared reading lesson. The teacher has asked Kim to work with a small group of
students who are reading slightly below grade level. Even though she is working
with a small group, Kim has decided to teach a shared reading lesson rather than
a guided reading lesson, because she wants to work with a grade-level text. Because Kim is working with only six students, the students are able to lean in from
their seats around a kidney table to see the pages of the book, so Kim does not
have to figure out how to enlarge the text or gather multiple copies.

The fifteen-minute lesson begins with Kim inviting students to share what
they notice about the cover and first few illustrations of the story, and students
periodically share their thoughts. After each offering from students, Kim summarizes their thinking. Then, she begins reading aloud the opening pages as students read along silently.

On the page that reads, "As soon as he reads one book, he brings home another. Soon the house is filled with books. His wife, Diana, grumbles" (2), students notice that Kim has covered the word *grumbles* with a sticky note.

Kim asks students to consider how they might figure out what word is beneath the sticky note. The students stare blankly at her, and Kim says, "We seem kind of stuck. Who has an idea of something we can try?" Kim waits for several more seconds. Finally, Morty hesitantly suggests that they could look at the pictures. Kim asks the rest of the group if they think that is a good idea. The other students nod and Kim says, "Let's try it."

The students move in closer to study the illustrations, and Nora notices the look on the face of the biblioburro's wife, Diana. They discuss how she doesn't look very happy, which draws their attention to the speech bubble above her head that says, "What are we going to do, eat rice with our books?" (3).

Concluding that Diana isn't very happy about all of the books in her house, the students return to the original puzzle: What word is hidden beneath the sticky note? Now the students have several ideas and offer possibilities, such as *complains, fusses,* and *asks.* Kim asks the students, "Without removing the sticky note, how can we figure out if any of these words will work?"

The students tell Kim that they need to reread the sentence with each word filled in the blank to see which ones make sense. As a class, they plug in each word and reread the sentence in unison, concluding that all three of the words could work, but it "probably won't be *asked* because that's too nice." The students are now completely absorbed by the work. Reginald suggests that the word could be *grumps,* but when they plug it into the sentence, several express concern that *grumps* "just doesn't sound right."

Kim reveals that the first letter is a *g* and the second letter is an *r*. The group revisits *grumps,* and students begin to wonder if Reginald correctly guessed the word. When Kim pulls the sticky note off and the children see the word *grumbles,* Marci pauses and says, "Oh, no! It's not *grumps*! It's *grum-bles!*"

Kim asks, "How do you know?"

The students point out that the letters don't match.

Kim asks the students to raise their hands if they recall seeing or hearing this word before and none of them do, prompting her to remind them to think back on what they've just done to help them figure out what the word means. Remembering that he had volunteered the word *grumps* as a viable possibility, Reginald rereads the sentence aloud and says, "I think *grumbles* is how you talk when you're not happy."

The other members nod their heads in agreement. Kim takes out a piece of chart paper and on the top writes, "When I am stuck, I can try. . . ." She asks students to think about what they did today as readers to solve the challenges in the text. As students reflect, they enthusiastically come up with the following ideas, which Kim adds to the chart:

- Think about the story and what would make sense.
- Do something! Doing nothing won't solve the problem!
- Look at the picture and notice the character's facial expressions.
- Guess the word by connecting several details.
- Look closely at all the letters to see if they match my guess.
- Reread the whole sentence to see if my guess makes sense.

Before the students return to their seats, Kim explains that because they are out of time, she will give the book to their teacher so they can finish tomorrow. She acknowledges the students' hard work and wraps up the session by saying, "Sometimes reading can be tricky, but working to figure out the problems is fun and makes you stronger readers."

Fifth Grade

In a fifth-grade classroom, Ms. Rodriguez distributes copies of a portion of Chapter 1 of *The Limit* by Kristen Landon (2010). She does not introduce the text or preview vocabulary, but sets straight to reading. Familiar with this shared reading procedure, the students use colored index cards to follow in the text as Ms. Rodriguez reads aloud. She reads at a pace that is slow enough for even struggling students to follow, but not so slow that her reading sounds inauthentic or student comprehension is compromised. She is able to monitor the students' individual reading by noticing the placement and movement of their index cards. The teacher reads the section where the mother is talking about "not going the frugal route" when she buys a new oven. The father responds, "Anything you want, love," going on to say,

"If a new oven's what it takes to bribe your mom into putting on a killer dinner for the Duprees, then that's what we'll have to buy her." He spoke louder so Mom could hear. "Order it right away, honey. We're going to nail that Dupree account. Matt, start shopping for a new bike."

"But I just got—" (10)

After reading enough of this part of the text for students to have something to think about, Ms. Rodriguez says, "So, what's going on in the story? Turn and talk to your partner." Since the beginning of the school year, Ms. Rodriguez has taught her students how to have discussions with partners. Each student sits near a permanently assigned discussion partner, so there is no quibbling over who will discuss with whom and no one is left out.

The students are accustomed to Ms. Rodriguez expecting them to do the heavy lifting of the meaning work during shared reading, and they have learned to think about the text deeply. As they summarize the text with their partners and hypothesize about what is going to happen in the story, Ms. Rodriguez circulates and listens in to their discussions. She notices that most students naturally reread all or portions of the text. She observes a couple of groups engaging in discussions about what they think the word *frugal* means. Several groups seem to have some confusion over the term *account,* although they all know it has something to do with money, as they know what a bank account is and the whole segment seems to be about spending money. A few groups seem to understand that, since the Dupree account and all the planned purchases depend on the mother getting a new oven, the family in the story is spending money *before* they actually get money.

Ms. Rodriguez calls on groups to share what they discussed. She is intentional about calling on groups who have figured out key points in the story. As the students in each group share what they have figured out, she has them tune in to their reading process and share *how* they figured it out. With them, she labels their key strategies and adds them to the ongoing chart of strategies for figuring out the print and the meaning.

One group explains that it figured out what the word *frugal* meant by reading the next paragraph, which says that the mother *is* going to order the oven with "all the bells and whistles." On the chart labeled "Comprehension Strategies," Ms.

Rodriguez adds, "When you don't know the meaning of a word, read on to see if the text gives you clues."

The students in another group share that they had to read the passage three times and that every time they read it, they understood it better. Many students in the class confirm that they had the same experience. Ms. Rodriguez adds "Reread passages or parts of passages to understand them better" to the comprehension strategies chart.

Ms. Rodriguez is careful to make sure that the students address all the points she feels are critical to understanding the passage. She does not, however, pepper them with questions that overtly direct their attention to *her* key points. Nonetheless, the students spontaneously explore and share most of the points she needed them to understand. They do not mention, however, Matt's statement in reference to getting a new bike, "But I just got—," which indicates just how amok the family's spending is going. So, Ms. Rodriguez quickly points it out. Then she asks students to find their place in the text and begins reading from a few sentences back. Once again, students follow along with their index cards.

Over the course of about forty-five minutes, Ms. Rodriguez repeats the process several times—reading aloud as students follow silently, providing time for them to discuss the text with partners, letting pairs of students share with the whole class what they figured out, labeling and adding strategies to an anchor chart, and quickly pointing out critical understandings students have overlooked. The students remain highly engaged throughout the lesson. Ms. Rodriguez has selected a text that immediately pulls them in and holds their attention so well that they complain when the lesson is over.

Shared Reading Reminders

- Get into the text quickly. Don't spend much time setting it up; let the book do the work. Remember, you want to begin with the end in mind, and no one will introduce the text in independent reading.
- Make sure all the children can see the words. This can be compromised by size of print, angle of the book, glare, placement of students, and so on. Remember, it is not a shared reading lesson if students cannot see the words and illustrations well.

- As much as possible, rather than directing students to notice what you have decided is important (conventional shared reading), use these open-ended prompts (next generation shared reading) to get students to look closely at the pictures:
  - What do you notice?
  - What *else* do you notice?

  This practice more closely mirrors what students will need to do when they read independently. If students overlook something you think is critical to understanding the book, ask them to look again while you wait. If they still miss something important, offer them a leading prompt, such as "What do you notice about where the butterfly is sitting?" or just tell them explicitly.

- As much as possible, rather than giving students leading prompts such as "Get your mouth ready" or "Think about what makes sense," (conventional) let *them* try different strategies (next generation) and figure out which ones work. Offer prompts like these:
  - What do you notice?
  - What can you try?

  Students of all ages will usually engage various strategies spontaneously if the text is carefully selected. Once they think they have figured out the word, try these prompts to help them reflect on their word-solving strategies:
  - How do you know? How can you check?
  - How else do you know? How else can you check?

  (Note: Don't tell students that they have figured out a troublesome word correctly. Let them practice cross-checking!)

- Create a running anchor chart where you accumulate the print and meaning strategies students use. Every time they come up with a new one, add it to a list. Make these charts accessible during guided reading and independent reading.

- After you work with students to figure something out, reread from the previous sentence. This practice reassembles the text to focus on meaning. Say something like, "Now that we've figured that out, let's reread the whole sentence to think about what it means."

- Keep the lesson pace lively. If students lose attention, adjust the pace by talking less and engaging students more, or end the lesson. Don't let shared reading lessons drag out beyond student attention. Stop while the lesson is still fun. If you end a lesson in the middle of a text, reread from the beginning or summarize the previous day's reading when you resume the lesson the next day.
- Sometimes, explicitly demonstrate how to use particular strategies to figure out words, word meanings, or text meaning. Again, remember to put the sentence back together and connect to the previous sentence once you have worked through the tricky part.
- Use student reading behaviors during guided or independent reading to help you decide what to emphasize in shared reading. Observe student reading behaviors—indicators of reading process—closely during guided reading and independent reading to inform shared reading lessons.

Next Generation Shared Reading: Chapter Summary

Next generation shared reading provides potent opportunities for accelerating students' reading. Conversations about reading processes can help students transfer reading strategies to their guided and independent reading experiences. Shared reading's engaging structure exposes students to the power of books and gives them insight and agency around their own reading processes, helping them claim reading for themselves. Like the students described in the quote that opens this chapter, shared reading leaves students "clawing" to read increasingly challenging texts.

Shared Reading Ideas to Try

- Use classroom newsletters, such as *Weekly Reader*, as shared texts.
- Engage in a weekly shared reading of a poem. After reading the poem together, give students a copy to add to a folder or notebook, where the poems will accumulate and provide engaging text for independent reading and fluency practice—not to mention help children grow to love poetry!

- Spend the last five minutes of a guided reading lesson engaging the small group in a shared reading experience with a text that is two levels higher. Meet with colleagues to discuss what you notice. How does this practice affect student enthusiasm for guided reading? How does it affect student growth in reading?

- Record (audio or video) a shared reading lesson. Review the lesson to reflect on how much work students are doing during the lesson versus how much explaining you are doing.

- Gather with a group of colleagues to examine the anchor charts you are developing during shared reading. Are there ways to make them easier for students to use? Consider everything from the way they are composed to where you hang them in the classroom.

- Figure out ways to extend the use of the shared reading text. Here are a few ideas:

  o Type up the text (copyright permitting) and let children reread and illustrate it.

  o Provide multiple copies to let children read individually during independent reading.

  o Develop a reader's theater based on the text.

  o Use the text for a guided reading lesson with groups that need even more exposure to read it fluently or understand it deeply.

For Further Reading About Shared Reading

On the Same Page: Shared Reading Beyond the Primary Grades by Janet Allen (Stenhouse 2002)

The Foundations of Literacy by Don Holdaway (Ashton Scholastic 1979)

Independence in Reading: A Handbook on Individualized Procedures by Don Holdaway (Ashton Scholastic 1980)

Scaffolding with Storybooks: A Guide for Enhancing Young Children's Language and Literacy Achievement by Laura M. Justice and Khara L. Pence et al. (International Reading Association 2005)

Read It Again! Revisiting Shared Reading by Brenda Parkes (Stenhouse 2000)

Chapter 4

Guided Reading: Reading Practice Under the Teacher's Watchful Eye

*M*r. Falker put a book in front of her. She'd never seen it before. He picked a paragraph in the middle of a page and pointed at it.

Almost as if it were magic, or as if light poured into her brain, the words and sentences started to take shape on the page as they never had before. "She . . . marched . . . them . . . off . . . to . . ." Slowly, she read a sentence. Then another, and another. And finally she'd read a paragraph. And she understood the whole thing.

— Patricia Polacco

Although Mr. Falker was working with Patricia individually rather than in a small group, much of the interaction in the excerpt above mirrors the work in next generation guided reading. In guided reading, the teacher steps back and lets *students* do the work of engaging their reading processes around a new text, just as Patricia does. The students invest their energy in the productive effort of digging into an engaging text as the teacher follows their lead. As the last opportunity along the gradual release of responsibility to watch students before they are released to independence, guided reading shows us how students apply all of their knowledge about *how* to read while we are still beside them to intervene if necessary.

What Is Guided Reading?

Guided reading is a small-group, teacher-facilitated learning session where students practice integrating reading strategies (Burkins and Croft 2010). During these sessions, students with similar reading levels and needs gather to read an "instructional" level text that has been carefully selected by the teacher for the particular group of students. Each student receives his or her own copy of the text. The session begins with a brief conversation about how to approach the text, which may be teacher or student led, and continues with students reading quietly to themselves while the teacher listens to individuals in the group read portions of the text. A guided reading session usually ends with a short discussion, recapping the story or the day's learning.

Unlike read-aloud and shared reading, during which skills and strategies are taught explicitly, guided reading tends to be the place where students work to *apply* what is taught, modeled, and practiced in the other instructional contexts. In guided reading, students work with texts that represent what they will soon be able to read independently, which means that the instructional focus is on the *integration* of print and meaning, with *students* deciding which strategies to apply when.

By asking agentive questions such as "What do you know?" "What can you try?" and "What else can you try?" teachers support students as they grapple with the problems presented by incrementally challenging texts. Students' productive effort as they puzzle through the challenges of slightly difficult text, combined with the encouragement and subtle guidance offered by a responsive teacher, helps them to stabilize and habituate smoothly operating reading processes.

This chapter highlights emerging trends in guided reading instruction that more closely align guided reading with independent reading, supporting student transfer of strategies to independent encounters with text. These adjustments to guided reading do not, however, render traditional practices irrelevant or ineffective. There will still be times when you will want to explicitly teach during guided reading.

Dancing Lessons as a Metaphor for Guided Reading

In our ongoing dance lesson metaphor, guided reading is the dress rehearsal, where students perform an entire reading "dance" mostly on their own. The dance has been choreographed, demonstrated, taught (read-aloud), and practiced (shared reading).

Now it is time for the students to practice the whole dance on their own, under the watchful eye of their teacher. As they rehearse the dance on stage, the teacher watches the whole dance from a seat in the front row. Facing the stage and removed from the dance, the teacher leaves the dancers to get a feel for working through the whole dance independently. The teacher rarely interrupts the dance to reteach the steps or offer tips to individuals, mostly taking anecdotal notes to help decide what to later review with the whole group or address in shared reading. This is the moment of truth and, with the impending independent performance looming (independent reading), students must identify and resolve remaining challenges mostly on their own. The teacher wants to see them integrate all they have learned so that during the "recital" they will experience success and joy.

Like Mr. Falker, teachers in next generation guided reading step back and allow students to demonstrate what they have learned by listening and watching as students make decisions about what strategies to apply when and where. Because teachers know that the reading that happens in these small groups serves as a dress rehearsal for what will happen when students attempt to read harder text independently, teachers pay very close attention to the problems that students encounter and watch to see what they do to solve these difficulties. Intent on helping readers become the strongest independent readers they can, teachers give students control of their reading, offering occasional encouragement but little advice.

Guided Reading Then and Now

Changes in the student and teacher roles in guided reading are substantial and prominent. With rising concerns that conventional guided reading instruction may actually create dependence rather than support independence, educators have begun looking closely at a range of previously overlooked factors that may contribute to student dependence. Teachers are making important adjustments that preserve the integrity of the guided reading structure while also requiring increased student agency and responsibility.

Conventional Guided Reading

Guided reading involves teachers working with small groups—usually four to six children—from a common text that is on the students' instructional reading level (Betts 1946). The lesson begins with the teacher offering a brief summary of the text as an introduction. He or she may also lead the students through a picture walk. Usually, the teacher introduces potentially challenging vocabulary to students, which alerts them to the difficulties they may encounter. Then, students read the text to themselves while the teacher listens to individual students read segments of the text one at a time. If students encounter difficulty in the text, the teacher offers specific prompts, such as "Get your mouth ready," "Look at the picture," or "Does that sound right?" After everyone has read the same text or portion of the text individually, the teacher offers a "teaching point" (Fountas and Pinnell 1996). The teaching point highlights a challenge the students encountered in the text and explicitly teaches students how to solve similar problems. The lesson usually ends with some discussion about the story.

Next Generation Guided Reading

Next generation guided reading, like conventional guided reading, involves students working in small groups from texts at their instructional reading level. Again, each student has his or her own copy of the text. What is different, however, is that the lesson is much less teacher directed. Instead, the teacher uses guided reading as an opportunity to understand how students' intact reading processes are working for them. More often than not, teachers do *not* offer a summary of the text or preteach vocabulary. The work of figuring out how to approach the text or noticing unknown words must fall on the students, and the teacher wants to see up close how students recognize and puzzle through such challenges.

As with conventional guided reading, teachers listen to individual students read from a common text as the rest of the group reads through the text at their own pace. If students encounter difficulty, teachers provide generous wait time and watch them to see what they will try. If students become truly stuck, the teacher offers general prompts that still require readers to make decisions, such as "What can you try?" "What do you know already?" or "How can you check?" Students may refer to anchor charts, which display lists of strategies they can try independently and that are usually developed during independent reading.

Throughout the guided reading session, the teacher makes anecdotal notes about students' reading processes and looks for patterns of difficulty to address in shared reading. The session ends with group discussion. Finally, teaching points are likely to focus on what the students *were* able to figure out, helping them reflect on and celebrate the strategies they used rather than focus on points in the reading that were problematic. Table 4.1 presents key points of comparison along guided reading's evolution.

Table 4.1

Comparison of Conventional and Next Generation Guided Reading

	CONVENTIONAL GUIDED READING	NEXT GENERATION GUIDED READING
LESSON STRUCTURE	The lesson is preplanned and often programmatic, the teacher summarizes the text before the students read it, and the teacher preexposes students to potentially difficult vocabulary.	Text selection is the backbone of planning for guided reading. The teacher is responsive to student interactions with the text as students independently figure out what the text is about and apply problem-solving strategies to figure out tricky parts.
PROMPTING	The teacher decides which strategy would best help students figure out the tricky spot and supports students with specific prompts, such as "Get your mouth ready" or "Look at the picture."	The teacher lets students try different strategies—which may or may not work—and encourages their experimentation by offering broad prompts, such as "What will you try?" or "What can you do next?"
THE TEACHER'S WORK	The teacher explicitly instructs through much of the lesson; there is extensive teacher talk and direct instruction.	The teacher facilitates rather than directs the lesson, observing students as they resolve challenges in the text and making notes about their reading processes. There is extensive student interaction with the text.
THE STUDENTS' WORK	The students wait for teacher direction and prompting. There is much listening to direct instruction, and some reading.	Students decide how to interact with the text. They identify and puzzle through the tricky spots in the text. There is much reading.

Why Is Guided Reading Important?

In the gradual release of responsibility (Pearson and Gallagher 1983), guided reading is the final point of support before students reach independence. In guided reading, students practice strategies introduced in read-aloud and shared reading as they work through the text mostly independently. Guided reading offers teachers the unique opportunity to observe students' complete reading processes in action, catch inefficiencies before they become habituated, and encourage students as they work.

Guided reading gives students dedicated time for reading practice from texts on the edge of their skill level. Practice with texts on students' instructional reading levels supports student progress along the text gradient as they apply strategies in increasingly difficult text.

What Makes Guided Reading Special?

A number of variables make guided reading noteworthy. With its location on the gradual release of responsibility—just before student independence—guided reading offers unique instructional opportunities. Here are a few things that we consider truly special about guided reading:

Guided reading meets students where they are as readers.

Unlike whole-group instructional contexts, which begin with selecting texts based on grade-level *ideals* for reading growth and development, guided reading involves selecting texts based on where students actually *are* on this continuum. In many classrooms, this is the *only* opportunity students have to read text that presents them with challenges on the edge of their abilities. Because guided reading is connected to a text gradient, it provides teachers a strategic way to lift the level of student reading.

During next generation guided reading, the teacher follows the lead of the student.

A strong guided reading session requires the teacher-observer to follow the lead of the students. While responsiveness to students may be challenging, requiring a lot of flexibility, it offers teachers the opportunity to let *students* show us what they know about reading and where they need to go next instructionally. We find that guided reading, with its small-group format and its precisely-ish selected texts, gives us remarkable opportunities to be responsive to readers.

Guided reading gives teachers an opportunity to identify and reorient inefficient reading processes.

Because teachers work with small groups of students with similar needs, observing and studying student reading behaviors becomes more manageable. Teachers are able to better understand and respond to students' individual needs in this context. During guided reading, teachers should engage in minimal direct teaching and a whole lot of listening and observing. Having time to closely watch children allows teachers to see how they respond to text difficulties. Documenting these behaviors and looking for patterns in anecdotal notes provides important insight into how children's reading processes are developing.

Guided reading (especially next generation) simultaneously works on all aspects of students' reading processes.

Guided reading is predicated upon selecting texts that allow students to practice solving problems, become more fluent, read for meaning, and build their confidence as readers. Because guided reading offers children time to read from texts that teachers carefully select based on student skill, it provides students ample opportunity to practice engaging their problem-solving skills. When children practice with texts well suited to their growing ability as readers, they can stabilize integrated reading processes as well as build strength and stamina.

Guided reading reinforces the importance of problem solving.

Guided reading encourages a growth mindset (Dweck 2006) and teaches children to embrace cognitive dissonance. It's the place where we allow kids to experience *not* knowing something while feeling safe enough to try new and different strategies to resolve the problem, usually successfully. Consequently, guided reading sessions communicate two important messages. First, not knowing is an important part of learning. Second, noticing tricky spots and trying to figure them out helps readers learn about how reading works.

Guided reading engages small groups in conversations about shared texts.

One of our favorite things about guided reading is that when small groups of students come together around a story or a piece of fascinating informational text, they are connected by a common experience. Because guided reading groups are small, everyone in the group can participate in text discussions. Reading the same text in close proximity to others allows children to exchange ideas and ask questions, much like adults participating in book clubs, which engages them emotionally and develops their shared history as a community.

What Is the Work of Next Generation Guided Reading, and Who Is Doing It?

In next generation guided reading instruction, students are doing most of the work as teachers watch them closely to gain insight into their reading processes and consider their impending progress towards independence. The work—which is the students'—includes deciding how to approach the text; identifying and resolving the elements that prove challenging for them; and identifying and discussing what they notice about the text, particularly if it is related to the text's meaning or the author's intent.

In order for students to engage in this intense work, teacher talk is minimized. Direct instruction during next generation guided reading occurs only when essential. Prompts during next generation guided reading are mostly general—letting students make the more specific decisions—and teaching points are reflective rather than directive as much as possible. To explain these subtle differences further, Table 4.2, illustrates the ways we tend to assume the work of students during guided reading and offers alternatives.

Table 4.2

Teacher Doing the Work vs. Teacher Facilitating the Work

PART OF THE LESSON	TEACHER DOING THE WORK	TEACHER FACILITATING THE WORK
BOOK INTRODUCTION	"This book is about a dog and a cat who go on an adventure in a big city." (Telling)	"How will you figure out what this book is about?" or "What should we do first to get started in this book?"
PRIMING VOCABULARY	"Before you begin reading, I want to point out a couple of tricky words in the story. This word is *department*. Everybody say *department*. *Department* means ... ."	"When you come to a word that you don't understand, what will you do?" (Implies that students will self-monitor and normalizes the need to clarify meaning when things don't make sense) or "When you figure something out, try to remember how you did it so that you can tell us what worked for you."

PART OF THE LESSON	TEACHER DOING THE WORK	TEACHER FACILITATING THE WORK
PICTURE WALKS	"Turn to page seven and look closely at the picture of the dog and the cat in the park. What are they doing?"	"I see that Jared is already looking at the pictures before he begins reading the book. That seems like a really good strategy. Maybe we should all do that and talk about what we notice in the pictures. What do you think about that idea?"
PROMPTING	A student trying to figure out the word *crumb* pauses or looks at the teacher for guidance. The teacher says, "Get your mouth ready."	A student trying to figure out the word *crumb* pauses or looks at teacher for guidance. The teacher says, "What will you do?" or refers the student to an anchor chart developed during shared reading.
SELF-MONITORING AND SELF-CORRECTING	A student misreads a word. The teacher says, "Does that make sense?" or "Does that sound right?" or "Does that look right?"	A student misreads a word. The teacher waits for the student to complete the sentence and says, "Try that sentence again." (This lets the student find the miscue.)
CROSS-CHECKING	When a student attempts a word, he or she looks at the teacher for confirmation. The teacher says, "Good job!" or otherwise indicates that the student read the word correctly.	When a student attempts a word, the teacher says, "Is that right?" and "How do you know?"—even when the student has read the word correctly. Then, without indicating whether the student response was correct or not, the teacher asks, "How can you check?" or "How else do you know?" to get the student to cross-check and confirm the correct or incorrect response.

What Should Next Generation Guided Reading Look Like?

In addition to the narrative description of next generation guided reading presented above, we offer this list of things to look for during a next generation guided reading session:

- Four to six students sit in a semicircle, each with an individual copy of the same text.
- Students problem solve, read, and discuss for almost the entire session.
- Students read the text at their own pace as the teacher listens in to individuals reading portions of the text.
- The teacher watches students work through problems and listens to them read and discuss the text throughout most of the session.
- As students work through tricky places, the teacher describes and names the strategies they use.
- As much as possible, the teacher provides general guidance—rather than specific prompts—when student processes falter.
- The teacher takes running records or anecdotal notes about student reading processes to help inform future text selection, group placement, and whole-group instruction.

How to Implement Next Generation Guided Reading

As with read-aloud and shared reading, optimizing the benefits of guided reading requires understanding the demands the text places on the students for whom it is intended, carefully observing how students interact with the text, and responding with just the right amount of support.

Prepare

There are three primary concerns when preparing for a guided reading session: grouping students according to like or similar needs, selecting an appropriate text, and anticipating the challenges the text may pose to students.

Group Students

Before any guided reading can begin in earnest, teachers may need to conduct an informal reading assessment to learn about students as readers and identify the level at which they will benefit the most from instruction. During this assessment, teachers should work not only to determine students' instructional reading levels but also to gather more specific information about their reading processes. When faced with difficulty in the text, what strategies do the children tend to use?

After assessing all of the students in a class, teachers make decisions about which students have reading processes or reading levels similar enough to place them together in an instructional group. It is very important to remember that these groups are flexible, and individual students will cycle in and out of them as they make progress or as their needs change.

Select the Text

The most important teacher work for next generation guided reading happens *before* the lesson as you are selecting the text. Text selection can make the lesson succeed or fail before the instruction actually begins. Select a text that will present some problems for students to solve but not so many that it will compromise their reading processes when reading. Students should be able to figure out most of the text's challenges with minimal, if any, support from the teacher. Most importantly, the text must be engaging for students! Their interest in the text will motivate them to persist in the face of the text's challenges and will give you a window into their active reading processes.

Anticipate Skills, Strategies, and Challenges

Become very familiar with the text students will read. Before beginning the session, carefully peruse the text to consider how it can support the developing reading processes of the children who will be reading it. This is paramount to successful guided reading instruction. Note the skills and strategies you'd like to observe students applying when reading the book. Anticipate and mark some of the problems they might encounter and think about agentive questions that you can ask to support students as they work to solve these problems, such as "What clues in the text can help you figure this out?" "What will you try?" and "How do you know you are right?"

Present

To begin, gather students around a kidney-shaped table, on the floor in a circle, or in another conducive space within the classroom. Distribute copies of the text and ask students to think about what they notice about it. Take note of students' responses and behaviors and, if needed, prompt with questions such as "What can you do to learn more?" or "What else do you notice?" Rather than plan an elaborate introduction, let students decide which strategies to try in order to orient themselves to the text. They may refer to anchor charts made during read-aloud or shared reading to jump-start their thinking.

Read

After the brief, student-directed orientation to the text, instruct students to begin reading. Primary-aged students may quietly subvocalize the text as they read, while older students will read silently to themselves. If the text is long, you may indicate where you'd like students to stop reading. It is important to note that during this phase of the guided reading session, students read at their own pace. This means that some students will be finished before others. To accommodate different reading rates, encourage early finishers to reread their guided reading book or to read their independent reading book until all of the members of the group have completed the reading.

Listen and Guide

Once students begin reading, pull up alongside each one and ask him or her to read aloud from where he or she is in the text. As each student reads, keep a running record of his or her reading and make anecdotal notes about the student's reading process. When students struggle, ask agentive questions, such as "What can you do to solve that problem?" "What do you know?" or "What else do you know?"

Gauge Student Understanding

Talk with students about what they understand about their reading. Support their efforts to think deeply and connect across the whole book. If students become confused or seem to lack the necessary skills or strategies to solve a problem, offer limited instructions based on your observations of their reading behaviors, but make a note about the challenge. If the difficulty is common among your students, wait to address it in shared reading. If it is limited to an individual child, address it as an intervention or during independent reading conferences.

Discuss

After all students have had the opportunity to read the text, engage the whole group in a conversation about the meaning of the text, the challenges they encountered while reading it, and the strategies they used to work through these challenges. The discussion during this phase of the guided reading session is usually very process-oriented, often leading up to a teaching point that is reflective (highlighting strategies students have used well) rather than prescriptive. Depending on the length of the text, in order for students to negotiate the print and comprehend deeply, a guided reading session sometimes takes more than one day.

What's Tricky About Guided Reading?

Guided reading is a sophisticated instructional framework. Planning and teaching a guided reading session without assuming all the work can be tricky. The following sections share some dimensions of guided reading that can prove challenging.

Grouping Students

Flexible grouping has long been a hallmark of guided reading instruction; however, grouping is a layered decision-making process that requires teachers to determine both *how* to group students initially and *when* to move them to a different group or a different text. While it is common to use reading level as the primary grouping determinant, we have found that thinking first about what we know about a child's reading process helps us create better learning opportunities for students.

Finding Great Texts

Because guided reading requires multiple copies of a text, it can be difficult to obtain enough copies for all of the students in a group. In next generation guided reading, this challenge is further complicated by the critical importance of providing students with texts that are highly engaging and that present rich opportunities for deep thinking. When looking for guided reading texts, remain dogged in your commitment to secure texts that offer meaning challenges that give students sophisticated opportunities to think deeply about the text as well as print challenges on the edge of their learning. This can be particularly difficult in beginning reading texts.

Thinking Beyond Text Level

When selecting a text for guided reading, it is tempting to simply match the text level to the current level of the students in the group, but next generation guided reading instruction is a bit more discerning and takes into consideration the particular needs, interests, and reading processes of the students in the group. This may mean that text selection wanders or stretches into surrounding levels in order to meet the specific needs of a group. For this reason, we like to think of group levels as a range, such as G–I, rather than simply as a single metric (Burkins and Croft 2010).

Providing Just Enough Support

"Instructional"-level text has long been the mainstay of guided reading. The term *instructional* however, can be misleading, because many interpret it to mean that text at this level requires a lot of instruction. This is actually inaccurate. In fact, even in its earliest inception, Clay described teacher support in guided reading as "brief detours" and noted that students must "quickly return to the main task of reading the text mostly by themselves" (Clay 1991, 199). In next generation guided reading, it is critically important to allow students to puzzle through their struggles and make decisions about how to solve problems without prompting, or even confirmation, from the teacher—neither of which will be available when they read independently.

Jump-Starting Progress When Students Plateau

Sometimes it feels as if nothing we do helps a guided reading group progress. In such cases, our instinct is often to do *more*—to meet with students more often, prompt more, talk more—but too much instruction when students are reading instructional-level text actually interferes with progress, especially when guided reading usurps shared reading or independent reading time. When students plateau, try doing more shared reading, experimenting with text levels, or finding more engaging texts.

Ensuring That Students Efficiently Integrate Print and Meaning

Students' reading processes give us windows into the instruction they have received. Children who "call words" but think little about meaning tend to have received a lot of instruction in the print system but little instruction in comprehension. Children who guess at words based on context without cross-checking with the print have usually had insufficient support in learning how the printed code works. During guided reading, our job is to constantly help children consider *both* of these sources of information, particularly noticing the ways the print and the meaning connect to one another.

Not Identifying the Text's Challenges for Students

When children struggle, our instinct to help kicks in. We must be careful, however, to make sure that the help we offer supports, not supplants, children's efforts to cross-check and self-correct. When we help children, especially in guided reading, we tend to shoulder too much of the burden of problem identification— which is critical for students to learn—as well as the challenge of problem solving. Unless children have lots of opportunities to practice noticing *and* resolving the troublesome spots in the text, they will not be able to read sophisticated texts independently. This does not mean, however, that we should watch students become extremely frustrated and offer them no support. Nor does it mean that we should never help students figure out where to direct their problem-solving attention. It simply means that we should wait, watch a bit more, and give students more opportunities to take the lead during guided reading.

Not Labeling Students

It is very easy to lock students into their reading levels, which are actually approximations rather than hard facts. Referring to groups or students by their text level is an example of sloppy language that can brand children, not to mention influence our mindsets about what we expect of them. Be creative and flexible in the ways you refer to groups. Don't hold reading level too closely; it isn't an exact science at all.

Misconceptions About Guided Reading

Because students read from instructional-level texts during guided reading, it is easy to assume that guided reading is heavy on instruction! Too often, we see guided reading lessons where the teacher has a preplanned lesson and spends most of the lesson "covering" instructional content rather than actually letting children read. More often than not, these teaching points can be presented during shared reading and supported in read-aloud. Then, teachers could expect and watch for students to actually apply the strategies in guided reading. Next generation guided reading should look as much like independent reading as possible because on the gradual release of responsibility, guided reading is just one step removed from independent reading. No one will direct students, point out tricky words, confirm or refute students' attempts, or summarize the text when students read independently. Educators often presume that, since independent reading is from easier texts, students will naturally implement the problem-identifying work that teachers model during guided reading. We do not find this to be the case. Students must practice the work themselves during guided reading.

Another misconception is that guided reading cannot begin for emergent readers until they have demonstrated mastery of a certain set of discrete skills, such as knowledge of all letters and sounds, left-to-right tracking, or familiarity with a body of sight words. That is a little like saying that five-year-olds can't join a soccer team because they don't know how to play soccer. Actually, these little ones learn to play soccer (and learn discrete skills) by actually being on the soccer team. Start guided reading early and support it with strong, explicit instruction and modeling in highly engaging shared reading, and watch what happens!

Cautionary Tales and Nonexamples of Guided Reading

Given the complexity of guided reading and the nuances of grouping students, selecting appropriate texts, and presenting teaching points, there are many, many ways to misinterpret and compromise guided reading. Here are a few common challenges and misunderstandings:

"Guided Reading" That Is Scripted or Prescriptive

Guided reading is designed to be responsive to a group of readers. Programs that direct the teacher's guided reading lesson may have some value as a place to start, but following any program strictly is certain to limit your ability to be responsive to your students. By offering limited text selection or scripted teaching points— neither of which can predict the specific interests or needs of your students—prescriptive guided reading programs defy the very definition and intent of next generation guided reading, no matter who writes them or who endorses them.

"Guided Reading" with High, Middle, and Low Groups Attached to Three Levels of a Basal Reading Series

This misconception is connected to the previous, but its effects are dubious enough to warrant specific attention. If you have divided your students into three groups and have simply given them the above-grade-level, grade-level, and below-grade-level texts included in your basal reading series, you are teaching traditional reading groups, not guided reading. *Above grade level* and *below grade level* are very broad terms, and there is a huge amount of heterogeneity among either group of readers. Most of the time, these basal supplements will not precisely match the needs of your students.

Giving Students Guided Reading Texts That Are Too Hard for Them

Much questionable instruction is taking place these days in the name of text complexity, but you must resist the urge to frustrate students during guided reading. Guided reading is the instructional context where students do the work of identifying and solving a text's challenges *mostly on their own*. If you find that you have to support children heavily during the reading—in other words, tell them what to do to figure out many things in the text—then the text is too hard and offers little opportunity for students to practice an integrated reading process.

Selecting Guided Reading Texts Based on Theme, but at the Expense of Level

If your students are studying simple machines in science, you may be tempted to try to find a guided reading text that is about simple machines. More often than not, however, classroom libraries and book rooms lack the expansiveness needed to support such content integration. Consequently, the teacher may select a text that is really too hard for the group and "scaffold" students by offering a heavy introduction, pointing out potential problems, and prompting heavily and specifically. Of course, such a lesson, where the teacher is carrying the weight of the problem identification, problem solving, *and* solution confirmation, robs students of opportunities to engage in productive effort, which is the very point of guided reading. While integrating science, social studies, and other content areas into reading is a worthwhile endeavor, during guided reading you must first remain true to the *reading* needs of the students, with secondary attention given to content integration.

Not Giving Children Enough Time to Interact with the Text

When teacher talk—particularly that which carries students through the text—dominates guided reading, then the teacher is doing too much work. This includes prompting when students are working to figure out a difficulty they are experiencing in the text. Resist the urge to jump in and prompt heavily as soon as students have difficulty. Part of figuring out how to solve problems independently—which is the goal of all reading instruction in general and next generation guided reading in particular—is experiencing the dissonance that comes with not knowing. Too much time spent introducing the text before reading or asking comprehension questions after reading can also usurp student reading time.

Round-Robin Reading During Guided Reading

Because the heart of guided reading is student reading practice, round-robin reading—when students take turns reading a sentence or section aloud as the rest of the group follows along—flies in the face of the true spirit of both conventional *and* next generation guided reading. Most, if not all, of the reading during guided reading is done by students who do so mostly independently and simultaneously, which allows each student to read the whole text on his or her own. This means that each student may be in a slightly different place in the text at any given point during the reading.

Going to an Extreme and Letting Students Get Frustrated

Next generation guided reading lets student responses to the text guide the lesson more than conventional guided reading instruction does, but this does *not* mean that we should never explicitly guide students during guided reading. Nor does it mean that we should not intervene when students are obviously frustrated. We don't need to throw the proverbial baby out with the guided reading bathwater. Rather, we need to work toward a balance of following and guiding students.

Classroom Snapshots: Next Generation Guided Reading in Action

The following sections present snapshots of three different guided reading sessions, each in a different grade level. As you read these, imagine yourself sitting side by side with the teacher as the books are passed out and students begin to read. Pay careful attention to what the teacher does to "guide" students during these sessions and think about how that may look different from or similar to the way you've been guiding students in small groups. Also, imagine yourself as the teacher taking notes about each of these students. What do you notice about each student's reading process (as presented in Chapter 1)?

Because the lesson snapshots describe next generation guided reading, they all favor instruction that lets student responses to the text guide the direction of the lesson. This does *not* mean, however, that all conventional guided reading instruction should be eliminated or that teachers should never support students with traditional prompts such as "Get your mouth ready" or "Does that make sense?" It simply means that literacy instruction has reached an extreme in the use of these prompts and that support in guided reading needs to tip in the other direction so that students can do more of the work.

Kindergarten

Mrs. Johnson gathers a group of three children—Veronique, Sunil, and Stephen—around a kidney-shaped table for a next generation guided reading session. She places *Little Blue Fish* by Lynnette Evans (2009), a level C book, in front of them. The kindergartners don't wait for the teacher to cue them, but eagerly pick up the books and begin to talk about what they see on the front cover.

Looking for words he knows, Sunil points to the word *little* and says it to himself without any prompting. He then scans the rest of the title and notices the word *fish,* but doesn't seem to know what it is. Meanwhile, Veronique chatters away about the picture on the front cover and says, "There's a fish swimming in the ocean!" When Sunil hears Veronique, he touches the word *fish* and says the word. He sweeps back to the beginning of the title and repeats the two words he knows in the order that he recognized them—*little fish*—and then quickly and easily points to and says the word *blue.*

Mrs. Johnson is surprised by how much the students do without any prompting at all from her and says, "Boys and girls, you already figured out so much without any help from me! I didn't even get a chance to tell you the title of the story. How did you figure it out so quickly?"

Veronique raises her hand and shares that she looked at the picture. Sunil says that he looked for words he "just knew," which prompts Mrs. Johnson to help him think aloud about *how* he knew them. "Sometimes it does feel like we just know words but that happens because we use clues from the print and meaning to help us do that. Sometimes we look at the first letter and when we think we know the word, we check other letters to see if they match what we think."

Mrs. Johnson points to each of the words as she reads the title aloud. The students chime in as she reads.

"Boys and girls, by now you already know the story is about a little blue fish and I want you to have as much time as possible to enjoy the book," she says. "When you're ready, go ahead and begin." The students open up their books and, as they've been practicing in shared reading, begin looking closely at the illustrations and tackling the first page of text:

> Little blue fish went swimming. He went swimming in the ocean.
> (3–4)

Mrs. Johnson pulls up alongside Sunil and listens as he reads aloud slowly and carefully, pointing to each word as he says it. When he arrives at the word *ocean* he points and says "sea."

Mrs. Johnson responds by saying, "When you read, you said 'Little blue fish went swimming. He went swimming in the sea.' Try that again, and make sure all your words match the letters on the page."

Sunil rereads, even more deliberately, but again says "sea" for *ocean*.

With a puzzled look, Sunil stares at Mrs. Johnson, uncertain of what he should do. She waits. After several seconds, he decides to read the sentences one more time. Sunil sweeps his finger back to the beginning of the text and again reads slowly and carefully. When he arrives at the word *ocean* he stops and says, "It has an *o*. *O* says ooooooo." After a pause, he says, "That word is *ocean*."

Not giving anything away, Mrs. Johnson says, "How can you check?"

Sunil glances between the word and the picture and says, "Fish swim in the ocean, so the letters and the picture match."

"You did it. You used the letters to figure out ocean and checked it by thinking about the story. What will you do now?"

"Keep reading?"

Mrs. Johnson smiles and waits, making anecdotal notes, but does not cue him.

Sunil turns the page and continues.

Second Grade

Mr. Oliveri places *Locked In*, a level H book written by Susan D. Price (2001), in front of four students who have difficulty with reading. They have gathered at a table for next generation guided reading. The students immediately begin talking about the image on the front of the book. Gianna pipes up and says, "I bet this is the father and this is the son."

Jabar chimes in that he notices that it looks like they are fixing something, and Katherine adds, "They probably are. It's called *Locked In,* which means they got stuck inside because the door is broken!"

Mr. Oliveri adds, "I see that you're getting your mind ready to read. I must admit that, like you, I was intrigued when I first saw the title and the cover. I can tell that you are curious, so when you're ready, go ahead and get started. Remember to use highlighter tape to mark words that you work really hard to figure out or sticky notes to write down your noticings and questions."

The four children settle into reading almost right away. Mr. Oliveri pulls up alongside Vincent, who has placed his finger beneath the word *parakeet* in the first sentence of text that reads, "Adam and his mom and dad loved parakeets" (3). Mr.

Oliveri doesn't say anything, but just listens and watches as Vincent attempts to say the word aloud: "par-a-ket-a."

Vincent looks to Mr. Oliveri to confirm if his approximation is correct, but Mr. Oliveri simply shrugs and says, "This is *your* work; try something."

Vincent begins to think aloud, explaining that he doesn't think that his approximation is correct because he's never heard of a "paraketa" before. He decides to read the rest of the page to see if he can gather other clues that will help him figure out the word.

He reads the remainder of the page and discovers that the word comes up again, but this time he has more information and tells Mr. Oliveri what he is thinking. "I know they're birds. And they come in different colors."

Vincent's eyes glance between the text and the word and he attempts the word again. This time he says it even more slowly than the first time. "Par-a-keet. Parakeet!"

Mr. Oliveri congratulates Vincent for sticking with something that was hard for him, and reminds him that using more than one strategy is oftentimes just the thing that readers need to do to figure things out. He moves on to Katherine, who is a few pages ahead of Vincent. When he pulls up alongside her, he asks, "How are things going?"

Right away, Katherine turns back to a page in the book where she has highlighted the word *birdcage* and says, "I didn't know that word."

"Did you figure it out?"

"I think so. I think it says bird-cage."

"How can you find out if you're right?"

Katherine explains that she remembered seeing the second part of the word on the first page that said, "The parakeets were in a big cage in the backyard" (3). She further explains that she wasn't sure of the word on that page either, but "it made sense that birds would be kept in cages and plus, that's what's in the picture, too."

Mr. Oliveri summarizes what Katherine has told him by saying, "So, when you came to this word and you didn't know it here, you looked for parts of the word you knew, thought about where you had seen it before, looked at the pictures, *and* thought about what makes sense! Wow! That's four strategies in one sentence."

Fifth Grade

Jan works with a group of six fifth-grade students as they read "Velocity," a poem by Billy Collins (2002). They sit facing each other, three students on either side of a table. They have read through the poem a couple of times silently, made notes about their thoughts and questions, and are now discussing the poem stanza by stanza. They began the discussion looking at Jan for confirmation and ending every statement as if it was a question for her approval, but by now the conversation is theirs, and they engage with each other without involving Jan much at all. Jan occasionally involves herself by asking questions.

They begin discussing the following stanza from the poem:

> the way it was breaking over the face
>
> of the locomotive that was pulling me
>
> toward Omaha and whatever lay beyond Omaha
>
> for me and all the other stops to make (12)

They are unsure what "Oh-MAH-ha" is. Cedric thinks that it must be a place because "he is being pulled there." Aman observes that a "locomotive" is a train and points out that the last line says "all the other stops to make." He goes on to explain that trains make stops at different cities. Tiffany agrees and draws the group's attention to the capital O in "Oh-MAH-ha," explaining that the uppercase letter could confirm their speculation that it is a city.

As the students get further into the poem, they begin to dig into its deeper meaning. They arrive at the understanding that the train is a metaphor for life. Cedric refers to the lines "as we rush along the road of the world" and "as we rush down the long tunnel of time."

Tiffany says that she is confused about the man who is sitting and reading in the poem, because he has "speed lines coming off him like he is moving." Others confirm that they are confused by this. Jan wants to make sure they understand what the speed lines are and asks them to draw the image from an earlier stanza, which describes a biker riding with speed lines. It is clear from the students' drawings that they understand the notion of speed lines.

They remain confused by the speed lines metaphor and the man who is sitting and reading. Jan offers more specific support by asking them to reread the stanza that includes the line "as we rush down the long tunnel of time." The group experiences a simultaneous aha, as several students make the connection between traveling through time and the speed lines around the man sitting and reading. Jan guides the discussion by suggesting that the poem is about life, death, and the passage of time. Jan asks them how they might further investigate this metaphor.

Aman suggests that they reread the poem with the theme in mind and mark any connections they see. Everyone agrees and they reread. In the discussion that follows, KeAndre refers to the line "before the time would arrive to stop for good," explaining that he thinks the final train stop is death. Tiffany agrees, reading aloud the lines "We must always look at things / from the point of view of eternity."

At the end of the lesson, Jan points out that there were three words or phrases in the poem about which they were unsure: *weak chin, meticulously,* and *Omaha.* Jan tells them the correct pronunciation for *Omaha* and *meticulously* and asks them what their plan is for figuring what each of the words mean. They decide to divide up the responsibility, giving one word each to three pairs of students to look up after the lesson.

Finally, Jan gives the students feedback on their agency, hard work, and resourcefulness. She asks them to reflect on the lesson. They all indicate that they would voluntarily participate in a lesson if they got to explore another poem in this way. They found the lesson "fun" and "liked being in charge." Cedric says that on a scale of 1 to 5, he would "give it a 100!"

Guided Reading Reminders

- *Always* make engagement and student interest the most important criteria in text selection; it seduces them into doing hard work independently.
- The titles of guided reading books usually are not leveled. If the title is not within the reading level of students, just tell them the name of the book. Don't let the title bog down the guided reading session.
- Give children time to solve problems before prompting them. Enough time often *feels* like too much time! To get a sense of how much wait time you are giving students, record (audio or video) a lesson.
- When children read a word, whether they read it correctly or incorrectly, don't confirm or refute their answer. Just say "How do you know?" and "How else do you know?" to get them to practice self-monitoring.
- If children focus on the print more than the meaning, teach them to look at the pictures on each page carefully before they try to read the words. Teach this intentionally and thoroughly during shared reading and expect it to carry over into guided reading.

- Rather than tell children to look at something specific in the pictures or in the meaning of the text, say "What do you notice?" Teach them to search for information themselves.
- Unless the book is very short or the group is very small, you won't be able to listen to every child read the whole text. Limit your time with each student.
- Connect guided reading to shared reading. Teach less during guided reading by addressing patterns of misunderstanding during shared reading.
- Guided reading sessions are short: fifteen to twenty minutes. If your sessions are too long or students are getting little time to actually read, you may be talking too much—in other words, doing too much of the work.
- If you have to talk a lot to get students through the book successfully, the book is probably too hard.
- Collect running records or anecdotal notes about students' reading processes as you listen to them read. This will make it easier to let them do the work and will give you a valuable record of their reading progress.

Next Generation Guided Reading: Chapter Summary

Next generation guided reading—independent reading's dress rehearsal—offers teachers an opportunity to observe students as they identify and engage strategies to resolve the on-the-run challenges a text presents for them. Though guided reading is critical, it has traditionally received more than its share of instructional time. By contrast, next generation guided reading—which can be used less often than conventional guided reading because it is thoughtfully coupled with intentional shared reading and read-aloud—can accomplish more in less time. Because guided reading is one step removed from independent reading, it is imperative that students take the lead when interacting with the text, just as Patricia did in the quote that opens this chapter. Teachers should step back to make careful observations about students' reading processes and intervene only when absolutely necessary. Thus, next generation guided reading involves less *guiding* and more responsive *following*.

Guided Reading Ideas to Try

- Push the boundaries of text level when selecting guided reading texts. Give yourself permission to let your knowledge of your students override the assigned level. If you find this challenging, begin by letting students work in the hard texts from one level below their current level or in the easier texts from the next level up. For example, it is often just as beneficial for students working at level K to spend time reading from hard level J books or easy level L books.
- Count to eight or ten in your mind before you prompt students during guided reading. More wait time gives them more time to figure out problems on their own. Let a colleague observe you and give you feedback on your wait time.
- Have someone observe one of your guided reading lessons. Ask the observer to pay close attention to how much time children actually interact with the text and how much time you spend talking. Explore strategies for increasing the former and decreasing the latter.
- Get creative about reducing the amount of introductory talk or instruction you offer at the beginning of a guided reading session. How quickly can you turn the work over to the students and let them begin exploring the text?
- Set up a system for regularly recording running records or anecdotal notes about each child in a guided reading group. For example, focus on one child per day in each group. Eventually, you will have a substantial record of each child's reading process. We find that this worthy distraction makes it easier for us to talk less and let students do more of the work!
- Establish a procedure for having children reread texts. Make this a routine. For example, beginning readers can reread the previous day's text at the beginning of each lesson, whereas older readers can reread a chapter for homework or during independent reading.

For Further Reading About Guided Reading

Preventing Misguided Reading: New Strategies for Guided Reading by Jan Burkins and Melody Croft (International Reading Association 2010)

What Readers Really Do: Teaching the Process of Meaning Making by Dorothy Barnhouse and Vicki Vinton (Heinemann 2012)

"Guided Reading: Then and Now" by Michael P. Ford and Michael F. Opitz, in *An Essential History of Current Reading Practices* (International Reading Association 2008)

Chapter 5

Independent Reading: Learning to Love to Read

*W*ith the wind in her hair, she read and reread the books about Tarzan of the Apes, in which another girl, also named Jane, lived in the jungles of Africa. Jane dreamed of a life in Africa, too . . .

—Patrick McDonnell

The mission statements in most schools include something about helping students become lifelong learners. The ability to independently experience the joys of reading, including knowing how to select and dig into a new text for their purposes, is our end goal for all readers. Independent reading is the pot of gold at the end of the gradual release rainbow, the place where students can discover their power and the power of books. Next generation independent reading requires attention to students' interest in reading, as well as to their ability to engage in productive effort with books of their choosing. It is where we give them the opportunity to discover who they are as readers, which can serve them their whole lives, as it did Jane Goodall, whose reading life is described in the opening quote.

What Is Independent Reading?

Over the course of read-aloud, shared reading, and guided reading, teachers explore with students a host of skills and strategies that students practice implementing with different levels of support from the teacher. Independent reading is the last step in this gradual release, during which students practice integrating these skills and strategies using self-selected texts that match both their reading interests and their abilities.

While independent reading often begins with a few minutes of direct instruction that reinforces a skill or strategy previously explored in another instructional context, it is mostly a quiet time during which students engage with texts on their own. During independent reading, teachers sometimes work with small groups. Alternatively, teachers may observe students as they work and circulate to have conversations with them about their reading.

Teacher-student conferences during independent reading may address a variety of topics, including but not limited to text choice, genre, comprehension, and interest. These conversations often focus on what students are figuring out about texts and how they have managed to solve the problems—tricky spots—they have encountered. Conferences provide opportunities for teachers to formatively assess how well students are transferring previously taught skills and strategies to their independent interactions with texts.

After students read independently, it is beneficial for them to have opportunities to share with one another some of the ideas, joys, and struggles that arose during independent reading. Encouraging students to reflect in this way can help build a reading community in the classroom.

This chapter addresses the special place that independent reading holds in the gradual release of responsibility. It also presents next generation approaches to supporting students in selecting and engaging with text on their own.

Dancing Lessons as Metaphor for Independent Reading

In this, our last comparison between literacy instruction and dancing, independent reading represents the recital. After watching the dance (read-aloud), learning the dance (shared reading), and practicing the dance (guided reading) under the gradually diminishing guidance of the dance teacher, students are on their own as they integrate every aspect of performing—posture, enthusiasm, choreography, energy, synchronization, and so on.

There are likely to be mistakes, but they are generally few and far between, as the students are well rehearsed and able to do most of the newly learned dance with automaticity. In the wings, the teacher may offer quick tips, words of encouragement, or pats on the back as students step onto the stage to dance on their own. The teacher, of course, does not intervene during the dance, even if students miss a step or two. Rather, the teacher watches the dancers closely and takes notes about their performance, observing their strengths and noting ways to fine-tune their next performance.

Most important, the students have the opportunity to get lost in the dance of reading—like Jane Goodall, who "read and reread"—and the teacher gets to celebrate their progress and their success. This independence is what they have all been working toward. Success breeds success, as students claim their identities as dancers. Dancing seeps into their everyday lives outside the dance class, as they dance around the kitchen or choreograph a routine to their favorite song. With the completion of the recital, the gradual release process begins again as the teacher and students figure out what they will learn next.

Like the dance recital, next generation independent reading requires teachers to give students a chance to read on their own, with little or no intervention. During independent reading, quick check-ins are like the high five backstage, and teachers make notes on the ways students negotiate the many aspects of reading. Because teachers have gotten to know their students well through read-aloud, shared reading, and guided reading, they look for confirmation that students are transferring previously learned skills and strategies into a seamless independent reading "performance." Any glitches in the reading routine, or troublesome patterns that emerge during independent reading, are noted and revisited in the other instructional contexts. During independent reading, the teacher can also think about what learning to initiate next during read-aloud.

Most important, teachers let students read, allowing them the glorious luxury of falling in love with books. This is what the students have been working towards. As students experience the joys of reading more and more, they step fully into their identities as readers. Independent reading becomes part of their lives outside of school, as they talk about favorite books on the bus or take the next book in a Manga series outside to read during recess.

Independent Reading Then and Now

Independent reading, as much as any other instructional context, has evolved dramatically. From the revolutionary days of "drop everything and read" (DEAR) to later evolutions of sustained silent reading (SSR) to its prominent place in the Daily 5, independent reading's permutations have at least two common threads: (1) some element of choice and (2) extended time to read. There are, however, some substantial differences between the ways in which independent reading has been used in the past to support students' reading growth and development and emerging trends toward practices that preserve the "independence" of independent reading.

Conventional Independent Reading

The heart of independent reading involves students reading independently from "just-right" texts. More often than not, the definitions of "just right" are specific and based on an assessment of reading skills. Typically, students may choose from bins or shelves identified with labels that match their demonstrated reading level or they may read an assigned text. Teachers may teach small-group lessons or conduct conferences during independent reading. The accountability piece during independent reading is traditionally high, whether students are writing summaries, recording their progress in reading logs, or using sticky notes to document their application of reading strategies. During independent reading, teachers conduct conferences during which they research (collect formative assessment data), compliment, and teach.

Next Generation Independent Reading

Next generation independent reading loosens its grip on reading level, expanding the definition of "just right." While helping students find texts they can manage independently is still a priority, there is often enough grace in terms of text difficulty for students reading above or below "grade level" to enjoy the classroom text. Students have some latitude to attempt texts that are challenging for them, and the conferences about these texts revolve around productive effort rather than text level. Students understand that different texts are just right for different purposes and are likely to be in the middle of two or three texts at once (Burkins and Yaris 2014). Teachers encourage students to think about the different types of reading they do and the ways different texts serve them.

The most important aspect of next generation independent reading is the emphasis on reading for its own sake. This does not mean that students never document their reading strategies or log the number of pages they've read. It means, however, that reading a lot of authentic texts for meaning and pleasure is emphasized above all, and there is a contagious energy about books and the things students are discovering in them. Students have an evolving understanding of their own power as readers and see problems as possibilities. Students are active and agentive in all aspects of independent reading, from selecting the text to reading for meaning. Teacher-student conference protocols are built around connecting, conversing (gathering formative assessment data), coaching, and celebrating.

It is important to note that, as always, there is a lot of variation across instructional contexts. While the preceding description and Table 5.1 present independent reading variations as two distinct categories—conventional and next generation—independent reading structures in reality may include more idiosyncratic hybrids of these two.

Table 5.1

COMPARISON OF CONVENTIONAL AND NEXT GENERATION INDEPENDENT READING

	CONVENTIONAL INDEPENDENT READING	NEXT GENERATION INDEPENDENT READING
STUDENT CHOICE	Students select the text some or none of the time. Students often read from assigned texts such as content area textbooks, comprehension passages, and other worksheets.	Students select the text most of the time. Students read from authentic texts such as picture books, magazines, chapter books, and so on.
NUMBER OF TEXTS	Students select one text at a time and read one text straight through before beginning another.	Students may select a few texts at once and may read from each (or some) of them in a single block of time.
TEXT LEVEL	Students are directed to select reading material from a relatively narrow band of text difficulty, which limits their text options. "Just right" is a single metric.	Students select texts across a range of levels; some may choose to read texts traditionally considered "too hard" or "too easy." "Just right" involves more than numbers; different books are just right for different reading purposes.
STRATEGY WORK	Teachers direct students to look for, and often document, instances of particular strategy use, such as visualizing and questioning.	Students identify (in conferences or in sharing after reading) the tricky spots they encountered and how they resolved the difficulty.
CONFERRING	Conferring protocols revolve around researching (gathering formative assessment data), complimenting, and teaching.	Conferring protocols revolve around connecting, conversing (gathering formative assessment data), coaching, and celebrating.
ACCOUNTABILITY	Students spend large chunks of independent reading time documenting their reading or their reading process in reading logs, book reports, summaries, worksheets, online quizzes, or other documents.	Students spend most or all of the independent reading time actually reading.

Why Is Independent Reading Important?

Given its place at the end of the gradual release of responsibility, independent reading is the point in the continuum of practice at which students integrate all that they've learned about reading and apply it on their own. From selecting texts of interest and appropriate level to monitoring their understanding to reading to clarify confusion, independent reading is the culminating event as new learning across the gradual release process is integrated into authentic reading.

Because independence and proficiency are the ultimate goals of all reading instruction, independent reading is arguably the most important part of that instruction. After all, if students can't apply previously taught strategies and skills independently, then to what advantage is our reading instruction? And how do we learn of the effectiveness of our instruction if we don't observe—without interrupting or teaching—students' independent applications of what we have taught?

In terms of benefits to students' reading processes, independent reading helps children improve their fluency, increase their vocabulary, expand their background knowledge, refine their interests, and build their confidence as readers. What's more, independent reading allows students opportunities to make decisions on their own about how to solve problems that arise in text, which serves to develop, stabilize, and strengthen an integrated reading process.

What Makes Independent Reading Special?

Because independent reading is the place in the gradual release of responsibility where students are "released," it offers many opportunities for both students and teachers to reflect on the reading process. Independent reading is special for a number of reasons, including these:

Independent reading makes students better readers.

The relationship between reading volume and reading proficiency is well documented (Allington 2011), and it stands to reason: the more time children spend engaged with text, the more exposure they have to problem-solving opportunities, new vocabulary, and information, all of which contribute to growing proficiencies in reading. In the same way you can't learn to ride a bicycle without spending a lot of time actually riding, you can't become a proficient reader without lots and lots of practice.

Independent reading lets students discover their power as readers.

During independent reading, teachers give students opportunities to choose what they will read, with the expectation that they will use what they know as they navigate the text. In order to have successful independent interactions with texts, students must exert effort to apply and integrate the skills and strategies they have been learning in other instructional contexts: read-aloud, shared reading, and guided reading. Ample opportunities to practice this transfer give students the chance to experience success, showing them the benefit of their efforts. Students feel empowered when they discover that they don't need help to read the books that interest them!

Independent reading reminds students that reading is a pleasure!

Unlike other times during the day when instruction and conversation are driven by the texts the teacher has selected, independent reading gives students the opportunity to read and talk about the texts that interest them the most. Giving children time to read for its own sake (versus for the sake of specific instructional standards) and to discover and discuss the books and authors they love helps them discover the intrinsic joys of reading. Positive associations with reading make the job of teaching reading much easier, as children who love to read usually read more and tend to be better readers. Such positive associations with reading lay the groundwork for students to adopt reading as a lifelong habit in addition to leaning in to increasingly difficult texts.

Independent reading is naturally differentiated.

During independent reading, students are encouraged to select books that match their interests and abilities as readers. This means that whenever students read independently, the majority of them are practicing their reading processes using texts that support their own growth and development as readers. Because reading conferences center around the reader and the text, teachers are able to assess and work with students as they interact with text on their level. No other structure or time during the school day offers such an opportunity to so naturally meet students' individual reading needs.

Independent reading gives students opportunities to make mistakes and to problem solve.

When students encounter difficulty during read-aloud, shared reading, and (to some extent) guided reading, solving the problem is a joint responsibility shared by teachers and students. In independent reading, however, the responsibility of solving the problem is the student's alone. This means that problems become opportunities for students to make decisions about when and how to use the skills and strategies that are being taught in other instructional contexts—the hallmark of the final step of the gradual release of responsibility. Such problem-solving opportunities not only reinforce the teaching and learning happening at other times of the school day but also serve to help students become stronger and increasingly independent as readers.

Independent reading provides teachers a way to gauge the effectiveness of their instruction.

During independent reading, teachers make observations about students' reading processes. Watching what students do well and how they respond in the face of difficulty provides teachers important formative assessment data about what students understand about the skills and strategies taught during read-aloud, shared reading, and guided reading. These observations offer a window into instructional effectiveness, helping teachers identify the places where they need to adjust their instruction.

Independent reading nurtures teacher-student relationships and builds classroom community.

Independent reading allows students opportunities to talk about their reading interests, passions, and struggles. Through both teacher-student reading conferences and small- and large-group sharing at the end of independent reading sessions, students forge bonds with other members of their learning community. The exchange of ideas about books and reading nurtures mutual feelings of trust and respect, which contributes to an overall positive atmosphere for teaching and learning. Furthermore, independent reading is an avenue for teachers to get to know students; it builds trust and gives teachers opportunities to make instruction relevant for individual students.

What Is the Work of Next Generation Independent Reading, and Who Is Doing It?

As the name implies, independent reading sessions involve students doing all of the reading work: everything from selecting the text to resolving textual difficulties. Once again, the work involves integrating previously learned skills and strategies, but this time it is for students' own purposes.

Teachers work with students mostly on a microlevel in guided reading, but in independent reading much of the teacher observation is on the macrolevel, as he or she watches the class assume responsibility for reading and gauges the general rhythm of the work. With the increase in high-stakes testing, however, it has become common—albeit unfortunate—for teachers to assume more and more control, even during independent reading. Such assumptions of control can diminish student interest and agency during independent reading and limit opportunities to authentically evaluate students formatively. If teachers micromanage independent reading, they limit student agency and engagement and, consequently, limit the amount of work students do.

What Should Next Generation Independent Reading Look Like?

As with the other instructional contexts, independent reading will look different in different classrooms. Certain essentials, however, are common. Here is a list of what you are likely to see during independent reading:

- Students read self-selected texts. Because they choose their books, students are usually very engaged. Thus, independent reading is mostly quiet, with the exception of spontaneous eruptions of laughter or gasps of surprise as books engage the students.
- Teachers take anecdotal notes about what and how students are reading.
- Teachers observe some students up close in conferences, but also regularly spend time watching the whole class to gauge patterns of engagement.
- The students may make brief notes about their reading process or about the books they are reading.
- Students read for longer and longer periods of time over the course of the year as they build stamina.

- Anchor charts developed during read-aloud and shared reading support student independence.
- Students are excited about books and are eager to talk about their reading lives.
- Students regulate themselves by finding a comfortable reading spot or position, rebooting when distracted, selecting texts, and so on.
- Students may be engaged with several books of varying levels during one independent reading session.
- Students may sometimes choose not to finish a book they begin.

How to Implement Next Generation Independent Reading

Teachers must attend to a number of details for students to reap the benefits of independent reading as a productive instructional context. From curating a wide range of texts to displaying supportive anchor charts for students to access independently to helping children develop stamina, investing time in facilitating the practical dimensions of independent reading helps establish a foundation that supports children as they transfer previous instruction into independent practice.

Prepare

There are many routines and procedures that, when established and nurtured, contribute to a fully operational *independent* reading period. Some of the routines and procedures you will need to teach students include, but are not limited to, how to check out books, how to manage books at their desks, how to settle into reading, how to read for longer and longer periods of time over the course of the year, and how to share and learn about interesting new titles. These instructional considerations need careful attention before beginning independent reading, and some will need ongoing attention even after independent reading is operating soundly in your classroom.

Teach

You will mostly teach reading skills and strategies during the other instructional contexts: read-aloud, shared reading, and guided reading. However, minilessons—very brief, explicit instruction—often launch independent reading time, giving students something to think about before they begin reading on their own.

To select a topic for your mini-lesson, analyze anecdotal records from guided and independent reading. This analysis may reveal which routines, strategies, or processes need revisiting in a mini-lesson. It's also important to develop mini-lessons that celebrate some aspect of independent reading that students are managing well and mini-lessons that include book talks, which model how to preview books and expose students to new titles they may enjoy exploring independently.

Read

Invite students to seat themselves comfortably around the classroom. Offering children some choice about where to sit serves to mimic the habits of authentic, lifelong readers. Adding pillows, carpet squares, or beanbag chairs to your library area or random spots around the classroom can help to make the prospect of reading independently even more appealing.

As students settle in, take note of the start time to help you gauge whether students are able to read for longer periods of time from day to day. During independent reading, the objective is for students to become deeply engrossed in their texts, so you may also take note of who settles in quickly and who seems distracted. These behaviors can provide important clues about whether or not students have selected texts that are a good fit for them as readers.

Confer

When students are reading quietly and you are not working with small groups, you can talk briefly with a few of them individually about their reading. Pull up alongside students to have conversations about the books they have chosen, to carefully observe their reading processes, or to touch base about the mini-lesson topic. Make anecdotal notes about the conferences.

The goal is to meet with as many students as possible each day (usually three to seven students) without substantially diminishing or interfering with their reading time. Conferences range in length, depending on the age of the student, from two to five minutes. Remember that conferences should be mostly conversational. When they become too heavily instructional, we tend to pull students away from actual reading practice for more than a few minutes, and we change the energy of independent reading.

Because students who struggle demand the most attention, non-struggling students oftentimes don't receive a fair share of conferring time. Keeping records of when and with whom you confer can help you make decisions about how to distribute your time among your students. Conferences also prime students for sharing, so remain alert to student insights that might benefit the whole class and ask these students to share their learning at the close of the independent reading period.

Share

Following students' independent explorations of books, give some students the opportunity to talk about their reading experiences. Sharing might involve students talking about the books they are reading, sharing something they noticed about their reading process, or connecting their independent reading to the subject of that day's mini-lesson. Sharing time builds community in the classroom, and you will need to explicitly teach students procedures for listening and responding to their classmates. Once again, documenting who shares will help you distribute sharing time equitably between quiet and talkative students.

What's Tricky About Independent Reading?

Although independent reading is conceptually simple, there are some common barriers to implementation. Generally speaking, allowing a whole class of students to assume control of their reading work can feel overwhelming for a number of reasons. The following sections describe some of independent reading's typical challenges.

Finding Enough Books

In order to read independently, students need books! Independent reading runs most smoothly when students have access to a wide range of books in their classroom. Stocking classroom library shelves with the recommended 1,500–2,000 titles (Allington 2011) takes time and commitment. Furthermore, these substantial classroom libraries need to be organized in ways that are intuitive and easy to manage for students. Build your library gradually, establish a check-out system early, and teach students to maintain the system as your collection expands. In the early days of building a classroom library, supplement the classroom collection with titles from the school and public libraries. You can also add breadth to a collection by shopping at yard sales, visiting thrift stores, and ordering from book clubs.

Helping Students Know What's Out There for Them to Read

In spite of the abundance of books available to children, many struggle to know what to select for independent reading. Regularly highlighting different titles by reading aloud the back covers, sharing short excerpts, or discussing what you loved or found interesting about these books can help minimize book-choice paralysis. These book talks also nudge children to read new authors and genres, thus broadening their reading selections. In addition, you can institute rituals where students lead book talks to share their enthusiasm about the different titles they are reading; this helps children know what's out there for them to read.

Developing Students' Reading Stamina

When students deeply engage with text for sustained periods of time, they enter the "reading zone," becoming completely absorbed by what they are reading (Atwell 2007). When students are engaged enough to focus on their chosen books for an extended period of time in this way, reading practice is both beneficial *and* enjoyable. Therefore, it is important to provide children guidance—modeling and practice—that builds muscle memory around managing their space, materials, and attention (Boushey and Moser 2014). The trick to building stamina, particularly for those struggling to maintain focus, is to stop independent reading while it is still engaging. Continue to do this on a regular basis, incrementally increasing the amount of time before interruption, until you reach a reasonable amount of time for the grade or age of your students. The ideal amount of time for students to sustain engagement during independent reading varies, with a general goal for primary grades ranging from fifteen to thirty minutes and a goal in intermediate grades ranging from thirty to forty-five minutes.

Protecting Time Allocated for Independent Reading

When the school week gets busy with assemblies, testing, classroom visitors, and other interruptions, time becomes a scarce commodity. Teachers have to make difficult decisions about how to use the instructional time that remains. When left to decide between read-aloud, shared reading, guided reading, or independent reading, it's natural to feel an inclination toward the structures that provide you more opportunities for explicit instruction—in other words, teacher talk. Though independent reading requires less prescriptive teaching from you, your roles observing, interacting, and collecting formative assessment data are as important as your explicit instruction during read-aloud, shared reading, and guided reading. Generally speaking, your instructional time for reading should be divided into roughly equal parts among these instructional contexts. If you lose instructional time for one reason or another, rotate the instructional context that is cut—read-aloud, shared reading, guided reading, or independent reading—so that you're not always skipping the same instructional context. This way, independent reading doesn't carry the brunt of the time crunch, and students have ample opportunities to practice integrating the skills and strategies that help them become independent and proficient readers. While we *do* recommend that you assign independent reading for homework, this homework cannot take the place of independent reading during the school day, as gathering formative assessment data during independent reading is essential to plan for future instruction!

Knowing What to Say During Conferences with Students

Reading conferences should be conversational and informal, yet they need to give you substantial information about students as readers. Usually, the direction of the discussion depends on how students respond to open-ended prompts and questions. Beginning with a prompt such as "Tell me about what you are working on as a reader today" turns independent reading into a teacher-directed assignment, and it makes the conferring conversation feel like an assessment. Beginning conversations instead with prompts such as "Tell me about what you are reading" gives you equally valuable information about the reader while maintaining a conversational tone and preserving the "independent" nature of independent reading. Conversely, a question such as "How's it going?" is quite conversational, but it's likely to get a predictable response—"fine"—that will require a follow-up question to get at more substantial information. A more revealing alternative, such as "What is this book making you think about?" saves time and is more likely to engage students.

When considering what to ask students during conferences, think about *your* independent reading and imagine someone posing each question or prompt to you. How would you respond? Does the question feel like an honest inquiry that fits with your intimate time with a book, or does it feel like an interrogation? Does the question make you think about your reading in ways that stir your interest and enthusiasm, or does it just feel like an interruption? Does the question broaden your thinking, or could you answer it with a single word or two? Carefully crafted questions and prompts help us gather formative data without inadvertently impeding one of the main purposes of independent reading: authentic engagement with texts.

Misconceptions About Independent Reading

The most common misconception we encounter about independent reading involves narrowing student text choices based on the assumption that we can closely align student reading levels with quantitative measures of text difficulty. Well intentioned, strict definitions of "just right" (and rigid adherence to them) can seriously limit student choice and ultimately rob students of reading energy. Furthermore, narrow or single definitions of text-level appropriateness are often unwarranted. Although there are some text choices that are obviously "too hard" for students and others that are obviously "too easy," narrowly or singularly defining "just right" tends to work against our efforts to help students learn to read proficiently, not to mention to choose to do so independently!

Too often, we encounter students who must select their independent reading from a single shelf that holds books considered to be part of their Lexile band or on their Accelerated Reader level. Unfortunately, this means we also see students who are very excited about particular titles being told they cannot read the book they are dying to read! We understand the impetus to help students find books that are presumably just right for them in terms of reading level, but there are other, equally important factors that define "just right."

We understand that the tension between level and student interest raises questions about the legitimacy of both perspectives. Rather than choose one or the other, however, we always recommend balance. Simply let students check out two, or even three, books! During independent reading, support them in spending some time in one book—perhaps beginning with the more difficult text—and then shifting to the other (Burkins and Yaris 2014). After all, this is the way most grown-up readers interact with texts. On a given airplane ride, we are likely to have a novel, a research article, and a magazine in our carry-on, and we will spend some time in each during our in-flight independent reading time. Imagine how you would feel if someone told you that your independent reading could only be from one text at a time, and all on a single reading level!

Another common misconception is that all independent reading is equal. The 10,000-hour rule (Gladwell 2008) implies that if we work for 10,000 hours at something, we are destined to be great at it. While those who become experts in an area *do* spend thousands of hours practicing, their practice tends to be efficient. Practice can make perfect, but *better* practice leads to more progress. If students are reading superficially—paying little attention to the meaning of a text—then hours and hours of practice will only make them better at reading superficially.

Because the nature of student reading processes—how well they integrate print and meaning—contributes substantially to the value of students' independent reading practice, it is critical that our work with students leading up to independent reading (read-aloud, shared reading, and guided reading) set them up for success. The only way to manage this alignment is to know students and their reading processes well. "If students' independent reading does not align to their work with text during read-aloud, shared reading, and guided reading, then we aren't actually following through with the last step of the gradual release. This often interferes with students' development of agency, and it limits what we can learn about their ability to engage in productive effort on their own" (Burkins and Yaris 2014, 131).

Cautionary Tales and Nonexamples of Independent Reading

There are many ways to compromise independent reading, particularly when accountability pressures lead us to believe that student-directed work may not optimize teaching opportunities around instructional standards. In fact, "independent reading runs the risk of becoming a casualty of standards-based instruction" (Burkins and Yaris 2014, 144). In the text that follows, we describe some common ways we see the potential benefits of independent reading diminished.

Reams of Data with Little Real Knowledge of Students as Readers

More and more when we work with schools, we encounter hardworking teachers with enormous binders filled with data about their students. They've usually collected data from a variety of online reading assessments, from district benchmark assessments, and from other objective measures. Too often, however, when we visit the same class during independent reading and circulate to confer with students, we find that far too many of the students are reading texts that are ill fitting for them or that students are only gleaning superficial understandings of the texts they are reading. To support independent reading well, we have to apply our knowledge of students as readers, gathered as we observe their interactions with text during read-aloud, shared reading, and guided reading. No online assessment can replace the teacher in this work.

Students Who Seem Excited About Reading but Are Really Excited About Prizes

Programs that test student comprehension of books to award points for reading are widespread. They are disconcerting, however, as apparent enthusiasm for independent reading is often actually enthusiasm for accumulating points and earning the associated prizes. Unfortunately, in the long run, these programs can impede student interest in reading (Kohn 1993), and the associated comprehension assessments, which don't typically measure deep thinking about a text, can systematically teach children to read texts superficially. Beware of shortcuts, such as these and other versions of paid reading, because rewards can limit progress toward the long-term goals you have for students. Ask yourself, "How well and how much will students read if the points and prizes go away?"

Teaching Students Not to Even Try to Read Books That Have Five or More "Hard" Words in Them

A beloved strategy for helping students find texts that are at an appropriate difficulty level for them involves teaching them to read a page from a text and count how many difficult words they encounter. If they encounter five or more "hard" words—either hard to decode or hard to understand—then they are to presume that the book is too hard for them. Though sometimes helpful, this guideline too often offers only a superficial gauge of a text's value for students, and it can contribute to the learned helplessness we describe in the introduction of this book. Difficult words don't necessarily make a text too hard. The *degree* of difficulty, rather, is the issue. If students engage strategies to figure out the difficult words, and if the work results in productive effort that does not interfere with understanding the text, then the text isn't "too hard." In fact, the text is probably optimal for student growth.

Assigned, Academic Reading During Most or All of Independent Reading

Student choice is at the heart of independent reading. With accountability pressures bearing down on teachers, there is a trend to make every classroom moment a teachable one. What is important, however, is not the teaching but the learning, and independent reading *is* a substantial learning moment. If we assign textbook chapters, practice sheets, test preparation materials, or even chapters of novels during independent reading, we diminish student engagement and thus student learning (Gallup 2014).

Teachers Reading Independently Through the Entire Independent Reading Time

In the earliest days of independent reading, "drop everything and read" (DEAR) gained popularity. Although many teachers have moved to interacting with students during independent reading, there is still a remnant of DEAR lingering in classrooms. Independent reading offers teachers the rare opportunity to observe and interact with readers in moments of true independence. There is no better time for getting to know students as readers, so we can't afford to spend it with our noses in a novel. While showing students that you are a lifelong independent reader is a worthy goal, you can do so by occasionally offering mini-lessons in which you share the books that you are reading and talk about authors that engage you. Preserve independent reading time for interacting with students and making anecdotal notes.

Requiring Documentation That Takes Up More Time Than the Reading

When we let the accountability aspects of independent reading take up more time and energy than the actual reading, or when documentation becomes the centerpiece for independent reading and dominates mini-lessons, conferences, and sharing, then we are letting the proverbial tail wag the reading dog. If your reading logs require a lot of detail, if students are summarizing or writing constructed responses for everything they read, or if you require an excess of reports, then you are likely teaching students that reading is just a school thing, not something that can serve *their* purposes. This is unfortunate on many levels, including test outcomes, which can be powerfully affected when students have time to read books of their choosing (Allington 2011; Allington and McGill-Franzen 2013).

Congratulating Students for Reading Hard Books Rather Than Congratulating Them for Hard Work

If we celebrate when students read books that we know are challenging, then we can send mixed messages. Like misconceptions about taking vitamins—*Vitamin C is good for me, so lots and lots of vitamin C must be great for me!*—students can assume that if hard books are good, *really* hard books are great. This can create a classroom culture where students look for the hardest books and you are trying to negotiate their text choice for them. Furthermore, it can create a fixed mindset—*all readers should read hard books*—around text difficulty. Instead, emphasize the hard work students do in books, which can create a growth mindset around reading: *readers who work hard get better* (Dweck 2006).

Classroom Snapshots: Next Generation Independent Reading in Action

The following paragraphs offer three snapshots—at the kindergarten, second-grade, and fourth-grade levels—of students reading independently and teachers conferring with them. As you read these, notice the ways the teachers give the students control of the conferences and foster student agency and enthusiasm around reading.

Because these conferences reflect next generation thinking about independent reading, they favor student choice and make space for independent reading to truly serve as the last stage in the gradual release of responsibility. Thus, teachers focus on collecting formative data by noticing learning trends and patterns across the classroom. Formative data can help them make instructional decisions during read-aloud, shared reading, and guided reading.

An emphasis on student independence does not mean that teachers never give students any guidance or individualized instruction during independent reading. It does mean, however, that teachers focus on gathering formative data while letting students actually read independently as much of the time as possible. Teachers preserve independent reading as a sacred, joyful experience.

Kindergarten

As independent reading begins, Ms. Sommers watches as twenty-two kindergartners take out browsing bags filled with independent-level texts—some self-selected and some from small-group lessons. Many take out their poetry folders filled with poems and nursery rhymes that they have read during shared reading. Still others read favorites from the face-out shelf in the front of the classroom or from among picture books the teacher has already read aloud.

The students quickly find their comfortable reading spots—a skill recently practiced until they became efficient—and in less than a minute, all twenty-two students are settled and engaged with their texts. Ms. Sommers watches and circulates, making a note of the start time as she gathers her notebook for recording anecdotal observations.

First she stops to meet with Artur, who has his poetry folder open to a copy of the well-known rhyme "A Tisket, a Tasket." As she moves in closer, Artur places his finger beneath the first word and in a singsong voice reads, "A tisket, a tasket, a green and yellow basket." Artur reads on, accurately maintaining a one-to-one match as he pulls his finger along beneath the line of text. Ms. Sommers listens until Artur has read the whole poem. She says, "I remember when you couldn't read that at all. All your practice is making you better and better at reading."

In her notebook, Ms. Sommers makes the following note next to Artur's initials:

> one-to-one matching; "A Tisket, a Tasket"; really loves
> nursery rhymes

Ms. Sommers continues to circulate and pulls up along other students, talking mostly with them about what they're reading and why, occasionally offering support as students need it.

Next, she scans the classroom and, on a grid with an alphabetical list of students' names that she carries in her notebook, she marks a plus sign next to those who she knows are engaged in their reading, a minus sign next to those who are obviously *not* engaged in their reading, and a question mark next to those who *appear* engaged with their books but about whom she has concerns.

Then, noticing that a few students have begun to disengage from reading and are poised to distract their classmates, Ms. Sommers ends the independent reading time while most are still engaged. The whole period, which was twelve minutes long (three minutes longer than on the previous day), still feels very successful. Before moving on to math, Ms. Sommers gathers the students on the carpet to help them reflect on what they felt worked well during independent reading time and to celebrate their growing stamina.

Second Grade

Fifteen minutes into the independent reading period, Mrs. Noriega observes LaShonda reading Mary Pope Osborne's *Dinosaurs Before Dark* (1992). LaShonda appears to be deeply engaged in the story as Mrs. Noriega pulls up alongside her and asks, "Will you tell me about what you're reading?"

Almost startled by the interruption, a smile spreads across LaShonda's face and she nods her head enthusiastically. She says, "This book is so good!"

"Isn't it wonderful when we find a book we love? You're making me want to hear some of this story. Would you mind reading a bit aloud to me?"

LaShonda quickly scans the page she was reading, places her finger where she left off, and begins to read aloud.

> Jack crawled through a hole in the tree house floor.
>
> Wow. The tree house *was* filled with books. Books everywhere. Very old books with dusty covers. New books with shiny, bright covers.
>
> "Look. You can see far, far way," said Annie. She was peering out the tree house window.
>
> Jack looked out the window with her. Down below were the tops of the other trees. In the distance, he saw the Frog Creek library. (6)

LaShonda makes only one minor miscue as she reads aloud. Her reading is fluent and expressive, indicating that she understands the passage, which matches what Mrs. Noriega already knows about LaShonda as a reader. Mrs. Noriega says, "You must be so eager to find out what is going to happen next. I won't keep you any longer."

In her notebook, Mrs. Noriega jots down the title that LaShonda is reading and the page number that she read aloud. Mrs. Noriega draws two balanced, integrated circles of a Venn diagram to represent that LaShonda's reading process is efficient, integrating print and meaning cues (see Chapter 1). She records that LaShonda's reading is "fluent and expressive."

Mrs. Noriega goes over to the bookshelf, gets *Dinosaurs* (Osborne and Osborne 2000), the more difficult nonfiction companion to *Dinosaurs Before Dark,* and jots a message for LaShonda on a sticky note: "You might enjoy reading this, too. It goes with *Dinosaurs Before Dark.*"

Fourth Grade

After a brief mini-lesson about how to return books to the classroom library, fourth-grade teacher Mr. Grant looks over his conference notes and realizes he hasn't connected with Steven yet this week. Mr. Grant gives Steven some time to get into his book; he observes him from across the classroom and notices that Steven takes out two books and puts them on his desk. From where he is standing, Mr. Grant easily recognizes the cover of one—*Diary of a Wimpy Kid* (Kinney 2007)—and notices that the other is considerably thicker. Steven looks between the two books, ultimately picks up the thick one, turns to the page marked with a sticky note, and begins to read.

Mr. Grant jots down what he observed:

> Reading a wimpy kid book and another really thick book; chose
> to start with thicker book; had page marked with sticky note

Then, Mr. Grant crosses the room and sits down beside Steven.

"Hi Steven. I noticed that you were choosing between two books. Will you tell me why you chose this one?"

Steven places his finger in the book to hold his page and turns the front cover so Mr. Grant can see the title, *The American Boy's Handy Book* (Beard 2001). Steven explains, "Well, I like to fish and this book has a part about fishing. It's taking me a really long time to read it, though."

Curious about why, Mr. Grant invites Steven to read aloud a portion that he has already worked through. Steven reads:

> The tackle necessary in this sport is very simple; it consists of five
> or six empty jugs tightly corked with corn cobs, as many stout lines,
> each about five feet long with a sinker and large hook at the end. (29)

Steven pauses and turns to Mr. Grant and says, "I didn't get that at first."

Mr. Grant responds, "What did you do to figure it out?"

"I reread it a few times. I just kind of took it apart and thought about what each part meant."

Mr. Grant asks, "Can you tell me more about that?"

Steven skims the text, rereads the line "It consists of five or six empty jugs tightly corked with corn cobs," and says, "Well, I like corn on the cob so I was pretty sure that they're talking about using that part that's left after you eat the corn. And then I looked at the picture. It shows that part being used like a cap."

Mr. Grant is concerned that although Steven read the portion of text with accuracy and worked to understand it, it is unlikely that he will be able to maintain such attention for the entire reading period. Mrs. Grant says, "We all have to work like that when we really want to understand something that is difficult. But it can make us tired. That's why it's nice to have an easier book, too, just like you have *Diary of a Wimpy Kid.*"

Steven nods and returns to his reading as Mr. Grant moves away, jotting notes about Steven's reading:

> Reading 2 books; working hard to understand Handy Boy book; switching to Wimpy Kid book when tired

Independent Reading Reminders

- Establish procedures thoroughly by explicitly teaching each aspect of independent reading, from how to check out books to choosing a place to read.
- Let students read more than one book during an independent reading session, particularly when the texts vary in difficulty.
- Guide student choices indirectly, as much as possible, through book talks, book clubs, and displays of books.
- Adopt broad and multiple definitions of "just-right" books, as different books are just right for different purposes. (For explicit guidance on this perspective, see *Reading Wellness: Lessons in Independence and Proficiency* [Burkins and Yaris 2014].)
- Stop independent reading sessions when students are still engaged. At the beginning of the year, students may only have stamina for five to ten minutes (depending on age).
- Let students reread favorite books.
- Make conferences with students a combination of scheduled conferences and spontaneous conferences based on need. This allows you to meet with everyone each week, yet also provides flexibility to address needs in the moment.

Next Generation Independent Reading: Chapter Summary

Next generation independent reading—the culminating event for literacy instruction across the gradual release of responsibility—provides students extended time to read texts of their choosing. Independent reading also affords teachers the opportunity to learn about students as whole readers, including their reading stamina, reading preferences, and the ways they tackle challenges independently.

With the rise of standards-driven instruction, independent reading is increasingly compromised, as narrowly defined reading levels and directives for documentation threaten to drain the joy from the very reading practice necessary to solidify students' integrated reading processes. Yet next generation independent reading—which is the backbone of independence—is requisite for students to ascend in text difficulty. Truly independent reading—the kind that changed Jane Goodall's life—offers an abundance of formative data for teachers while also teaching students to love reading as a way of life.

Independent Reading Ideas to Try

- Widen students' reading worlds by talking to them about the different kinds of reading you do. Take in a selection of texts—for example, magazines, novels, informational texts, and newspapers—and talk with students about the ways each item is just right for you.
- Build classroom community by letting students solve together the problems that arise during independent reading. Traffic to the library too distracting? Students arguing over a favorite title? The biography bin gone missing? Use mini-lesson time to engage students in conversations about ways to solve the problem.
- Document the feedback you give students during independent reading. What percentage is directive and what percentage prompts them to reflect on their reading processes? With the support of colleagues, explore ways to shift these percentages so that more of your conferences are celebration oriented. Document your progress over time.
- Let students take the lead in independent reading conferences whenever it seems appropriate. Sometimes, rather than teaching something, ask questions that will give you insight into student learning, such as "What are you thinking about?" or "Why did you choose this book?"

For Further Reading About Independent Reading

Reading Wellness: Lessons in Independence and Proficiency by Jan Burkins and Kim Yaris (Stenhouse 2014)

The Daily 5: Fostering Literacy Independence in the Elementary Grades (2nd Edition) by Gail Boushey and Joan Moser (Stenhouse 2014)

The Book Whisperer: Awakening the Inner Reader in Every Child by Donalyn Miller (Jossey-Bass 2009)

The Reading Zone: How to Help Kids Become Skilled, Passionate, Habitual, Critical Readers by Nancie Atwell (Scholastic 2007)

Readers Front and Center: Helping All Students Engage with Complex Text by Dorothy Barnhouse (Stenhouse 2014)

Summer Reading: Closing the Rich/Poor Reading Achievement Gap by Richard Allington and Anne McGill-Franzen (Teachers College Press 2013)

Chapter 6

Putting It All Together

*T*he brain that does the work is the brain that does the learning.
—David Sousa

Sugata Mitra, a professor of educational technology in Newcastle, England, is interested in self-organized learning systems. Through the years, he has conducted numerous studies and experiments to better understand scaffolding, specifically, how much support children need in order to maximize their productive effort, or hard work that results in success rather than frustration.

In one experiment, Mitra (2010) placed computer kiosks equipped with high-speed Internet in some of the poorest and most remote locations in India. The children in these areas had little to no schooling and had never before used a computer. He turned the computers on and, using remote screen-viewing software, he waited to see what the children would do with them.

Naturally, the children were curious. They gathered around the kiosks in groups and started clicking buttons. In one village, within four hours of seeing the computer for the first time, children figured out how to record their own music and play it back. In another village, within fourteen days of encountering the computer kiosk, children learned how to download and watch videos from the Internet. New information spread like wildfire—when one group figured something out, they taught children in other groups what they had learned, which accelerated the pace of new discoveries. And what's more, the children did this independently.

The results were so impressive that Mitra began to wonder what would happen if he gave the children something difficult to figure out—the science of DNA replication. After giving students two months to work with software that teaches DNA replication science, he asked them what they had learned. They told him that they had worked on it every day and that "apart from the fact that imperfect replication of the DNA molecule causes genetic disease, we don't get it." Obviously, the students had learned a lot! They had not learned, however, as much as the control-group students, who were from an affluent area of New Delhi and were receiving instruction from a trained biologist.

So, Mitra decided that the village children needed a teacher, too. He had to make sure the teacher let the children continue to do as much of the work as possible on their own. So, he taught her to use the "grandmother method." He told her to stand behind the children and every time they figured something out say, "Wow! How did you do that?" and "What will you do now?" Amazingly, after two months with the grandmother method, the village children's scores jumped to match those of the affluent, urban students studying under a trained biologist.

In education, it is easy to find lots of directions about how to scaffold students. There are whole books about conferring, gathering data, and differentiating instruction. Publishers even sell thirty-seven-page prompting guides that tell us the precise cues to use as children work to solve particular problems during their interactions with text. While these resources offer some valuable information and our teaching has been positively influenced by some of them, we also believe that education could use a little more of the grandmother method.

Consider the following interaction with a student, which Lyons, Pinnell, and DeFord (1993) offer as an instructional *nonexample* in *Partners in Learning: Teachers and Children in Reading Recovery*. This exchange between the teacher (Bill) and the student (Peter) is around the student's negotiations of a tricky spot in *Rosie's Walk* (Hutchins 1968) and illustrates the type of heavy scaffolding we often see in classrooms.

> Bill: You worked hard on this page. Where was the tricky part?
>
> [*The student points to the word* through.] Look at the picture and tell me what she did.
>
> Peter: She went over the fence.
>
> Bill: It could be *over*, but check to see if what you read looks right.
>
> Peter: No, it's not *over*.
>
> Bill: How do you know?
>
> Peter: There's no *v*.

Bill: Good checking. What would make sense?

Peter: I don't know.

Bill: Would *through* make sense?

Peter: Oh, yea— "through the fence." (162–163)

If you look closely at this exchange, you will notice several places where the teacher is taking over the work of the student. Unlike the grandmother method, in which the teacher asks reflective questions such as "How did you do that?" our traditional prompts are much more heavy-handed. We tend to err toward the opposite extreme, offering very specific guidance with very little wait time. Educators understandably want to avoid frustrating students! When we preempt student efforts and give them little time to muddle through the tricky parts on their own, however, we minimize their opportunities for productive effort.

What if there is a happy medium—somewhere between taking on most of the work ourselves and leaving students to weep over their books? What if we simply prompted students to rely on themselves and on the text a little bit more, and to lean on us a little bit less?

In contrast to the lesson with Bill and Peter, above, consider the alternative, which is a revised version of this teacher/student interaction:

Teacher: You worked hard on this page. Where was the tricky part?

[*The student points to the word* through.] What could you try?

Student: Looking at the letters.

Teacher: Did you try that?

Peter: No. [*Student looks at teacher and waits.*]

Teacher: You have to try something. [*Teacher looks at student and waits.*]

Student: [*Tries to decode the word.*] th-r-ō, throw

Teacher: How did that work?

Student: It's not right.

Teacher: How do you know?

Student: It doesn't make sense. "She went *throw* the fence." [*Student pauses.*] It's *through*! She went *through* the fence.

Teacher: Are you sure? How do you know?

Student: [*Looks at the picture.*] Well, at first I thought she was going *over* the fence, but the word starts with thr- and in the picture she's not going over the fence, she's going through it.

Teacher: Way to make sure the words and the story match, just the way we practiced in shared reading! Your hard work is making you a better and better reader.

Look closely at the work of the teacher and the work of the student in the revised exchange. Notice how the teacher nudges the student to lean in to the work. The teacher neither lets the student flounder nor tells the student exactly what to do. The teacher intentionally uses language that communicates confidence that the student can and will do the work in the text. This thoughtful language, though much more general than traditional prompting, is more likely to lead to maximum productive effort from the student.

Minimal Teacher Scaffolding, Maximum Student Productive Effort

Recently, Kim's seventh-grade son, Nathan, called her with a homework problem while she was away on business. His English teacher had assigned an article to read about the neuroscience of magic and he didn't "get it." Because he didn't get it, he was unable to complete the assignment: summarizing the article paragraph by paragraph.

Had Kim been at home, her first instinct would have been to look at the article to assess the situation. She would have seen that the article Nathan was working with was indeed difficult! Because the text was hard, Kim's next instinct would have been to engage Nathan in shared reading, sitting him down next to her and reading the text aloud with him as he followed along and joined in when he could. She would have made most of the decisions about how quickly or slowly to read the text, when to stop, and where to reread. However, Kim couldn't offer any of this substantive scaffolding because she wasn't even in the same town. She was at the mercy of circumstance, and in this circumstance, the only thing she knew to say was, "I'll listen as you read it aloud, and if you get in over your head, I will do what I can to help you help yourself." Basically, Kim inadvertently ended up engaging Nathan in the equivalent of guided reading.

When Nathan encountered words he didn't know as he read aloud, such as *subtly* and *cognitive,* Kim asked him, "What are you going to do to figure it out?" With the first few words, he wanted to quit, but he would inevitably say something like, "I don't know . . . reread, I guess" and figure out the word. With his building success, he began to lean in to the work. His feelings of defeat quickly morphed to determination. He became intent on figuring out what this really hard text was saying—he made wise decisions about how to pace his reading, how to chunk the text, and when to reread. When he got things right, Kim—inadvertently employing the grandmother method—said, "Wow! What's next?" and little by little, Nathan cobbled together an understanding of the article, which deepened as he reread sections and talked about the meaning with Kim.

Kim couldn't see Nathan, but she could hear growing confidence in his voice each time he figured something out. Naturally, Kim was excited for him, but she was also humbled. Had she been at home, Kim never would have learned how much Nathan was capable of because she would have assumed a lot of the work.

This story touches the very heart of *Who's Doing the Work?*—scaffolding in ways that maximize children's learning so that they can become increasingly independent. As teachers, we are faced daily with multiple decisions about how much and what kind of support to offer children, and about which instructional contexts to implement when. Oftentimes, we worry that if we don't support enough, students will become frustrated, disengaged, and unmotivated. However, in our efforts to support students, it seems we forget that *some* struggle is an important part of engaged learning. The key, as we describe in *Reading Wellness,* is productive effort.

> Once students understand the *types* of problems they encounter as they read—as well as the productive effort they put forth to solve them—improving their ability to face increasingly challenging text, then many problems become opportunities to get stronger, rather than reasons to choose a different book. Recasting decoding or comprehension "problems"—tricky parts—as possibilities, can change the work and bring new energy to reading tasks, whether they are shared, guided, or independent. (Burkins and Yaris 2014, 122)

When we intervene too soon, offer too much support, or mismatch the text with the instructional context (think of Kim, who would have supported Nathan through shared reading rather than guided reading), we rob students of learning opportunities. Furthermore, if we overscaffold, students can become dependent, disinterested, and unmotivated.

Of course, underscaffolding has its own serious consequences (Burkins and Croft 2010), causing frustration and creating inefficient reading habits as students learn to overrely on their strongest strategies and neglect the development of other, equally important skills and strategies. Reading texts that are too hard too often can seriously thwart students' development of a smoothly operating, efficient reading process.

Next generation scaffolding aims to find a happy medium between under- and overscaffolding. It optimizes the benefits of both the grandmother method and traditional prompting. It involves making informed decisions about how to intentionally support students by scaffolding in ways that consider the students, the texts, and the task in order to maximize productive effort.

Next Generation Scaffolding

Part of the productive effort required to learn to read involves interacting with text and working through difficulties. As children engage with texts, as Nathan did reading the article on the neuroscience of magic, they have three primary sources of support: themselves, the text, and the teacher (see Figure 6.1).

Figure 6.1

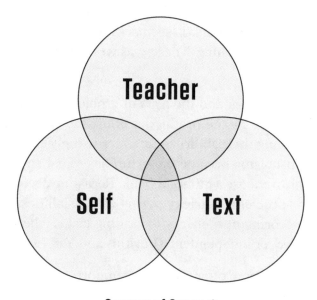

Sources of Support

Historically, our scaffolding across instructional contexts has been teacher-heavy. Consider Kim's initial reaction to Nathan's pleas for support. Had Kim been at home with her son, she would have overscaffolded him, forcing him to rely more on her than on the text or himself. The overscaffolding model is represented by the Venn diagram in Figure 6.2.

Figure 6.2

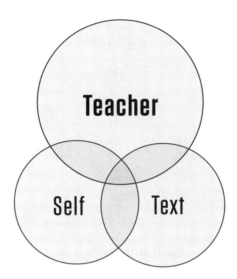

Sources of Support with Teacher Role Maximized

Next generation instruction scaffolds differently regardless of instructional context, shifting the teacher's role from one of primary support to one that prompts students to look to the text and to themselves to figure out *how* to do the work. Like Kim's support of Nathan as he read and summarized his assigned article, next generation reading instruction moves in the direction of the grandmother method; it reserves the right to offer heavier, more specific support, but generally minimizes the teacher's role as much as possible. Next generation scaffolding is illustrated in Figure 6.3.

Part of the challenge, which is also part of the fun, is keeping our eyes on the end goal of our instruction—students habituating integrated strategies that maximize productive effort. There are three primary goals as we teach across the gradual release of responsibility: to minimize the teacher role, to maximize productive student work, and to teach for transfer. We explore these three dimensions of instruction by considering teacher language, text selection, and instructional context in the sections that follow. The ideas in these sections overlap quite a lot, but we have parsed them out so that we can examine each more closely, as well as explore the connections among them.

Figure 6.3

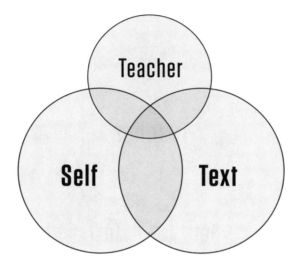

Sources of Support with Teacher Role Minimized

Teacher Language and Maximizing the Student Role

Our instructional language can help minimize the teacher role, as shown in the Venn diagram in Figure 6.3. In particular, the prompts we choose to use with students and the ways we talk about their interactions with text can assume or release responsibility for the reading work. Specific or directive prompts, although sometimes necessary, eliminate opportunities for students to engage in productive effort. As much as possible, prompts that help students think about the tricky parts of the text, reflect on their reading process, and follow generous wait time should precede your use of more specific prompts, which tend to limit productive effort. Figure 6.4 provides a hierarchy of prompts to consider when working with students.

Figure 6.4

THE PROMPTING FUNNEL

1. Look To Self

What can you try?

What do you know? (background knowledge)

Wow! How did you do that?

How can you check?

Explain.

2. Look to Text

What can you use?

What do you know? (from the text)

Where is the tricky part?

What can you figure out?

Show me.

3. Look to Teacher

Get your mouth ready.

Does that make sense?

Does that sound right?

Look at the picture.

Reread.

The prompts near the top of the funnel move children toward independence, as looking to oneself and to the text are problem-solving options students can use even when a teacher is not present. The prompts at the bottom of the funnel explicitly direct student action and, over time, teach students to wait for teachers to tell them exactly what to do when they are stuck. While there are situations in which it may be appropriate to use the more specific prompts shown at the bottom of the funnel, their placement indicates that we should use them as a last resort. When deciding what to say as students are problem solving in texts across the instructional contexts, ask yourself: If I use this prompt, will I eliminate work that students could do themselves?

Text Level and Maximizing the Student Role

Text selection is the most important scaffolding work you will do for students. Locating texts that lure students into reading will inadvertently lead them to shoulder more of the work across the gradual release of responsibility. Texts need to be difficult enough, but not too difficult, given the teacher role in each instructional context. Finding a match between students and text involves subtleties that are not measured by quantitative leveling systems. Furthermore, different levels of text are just right for different children in different contexts (Burkins and Yaris 2014). Nevertheless, Table 6.1 summarizes general guidelines for consideration as you select texts for each instructional context.

Table 6.1

INSTRUCTIONAL CONTEXTS AND TEXT LEVELS

INSTRUCTIONAL CONTEXT	TEXT LEVEL
READ-ALOUD	Substantially above grade level or at the average listening comprehension level of the group
SHARED READING	On or a little above grade level or just beyond the average reading level of the group
GUIDED READING	On group's instructional reading level
INDEPENDENT READING	On reader's individual independent reading level

As you select texts, keep in mind that texts, students, and tasks are idiosyncratic. Your knowledge of your students trumps any guidelines. There is a lot of flexibility in text selection, as was demonstrated when Kim supported her son, Nathan, in a guided reading context as he shouldered the bulk of the work in a text that was difficult for him. If Nathan spent all his time in texts this difficult or without the guided support of a teacher, however, he would likely grow frustrated, habituate a compromised reading process, and lose interest in reading. Nathan also needs to read books that are just right for him in different contexts.

People magazine and *Theoretical Models and Processes of Reading* (Alvermann, Unrau, and Ruddell 2013) are very different in terms of how hard we have to work to understand them, but both are just right for us. We would hate, however, for someone to say that we could *only* read one or the other of these texts! Similarly, your determinations of a text's just-right-ness in a particular lesson or for a particular reader will depend on the instructional context and on the needs of your students. When selecting a text, ask yourself: Is this text engaging enough, difficult enough, *and* manageable enough for students to experience optimum productive effort?

Instructional Context and Maximizing the Student Role

All the different instructional contexts we describe in this book—read-aloud, shared reading, guided reading, and independent reading—are equally important because they each offer students experiences with different levels of text. When you understand the role of each instructional context, the work of text selection and of scaffolding becomes clearer, and you are better able to develop lessons that engage students in doing as much of the work as possible. Table 6.2 details the role the teacher and the student typically play in read-aloud, shared reading, guided reading, and independent reading.

Table 6.2

CHARACTERISTICS OF INSTRUCTIONAL CONTEXTS

INSTRUCTIONAL CONTEXT	CHARACTERISTICS OF THE WORK
READ-ALOUD	• Only the teacher has a copy of the text. • Children access sophisticated text without any print limitations. • Focus is on meaning, which is made by students but supported by teachers. • Teacher models the messy comprehension-monitoring behaviors that students will apply during shared reading, guided reading, and independent reading. • Experience is pleasurable and engaging, even fun.

INSTRUCTIONAL CONTEXT	CHARACTERISTICS OF THE WORK
SHARED READING	• Students and teacher have access to the text. • Students and teacher share the work of integrating print and meaning. • Discussion is heavy in reading process language so that students can see how print and meaning overlap to help them understand the story. • Teacher may record student learning on anchor chart to support transfer of integrated strategies into guided and independent reading. • Lessons are drawn from observations about student reading processes in guided and independent reading. • Experience is pleasurable and engaging, even fun.
GUIDED READING	• Students and teacher have access to the text. • Students do most of the work of integrating print and meaning. Teacher offers students support through prompting that cues them to figure out what to do. • Students practice integrated strategies previously taught and practiced in shared reading. • Students refer to the anchor charts as appropriate. • Teachers mostly observe, gathering formative assessment data to inform work in other instructional contexts. • Experience is pleasurable and engaging, even fun.
INDEPENDENT READING	• Only students have access to the text; teachers may look on. • Students do all the work of integrating print and meaning. • Students may refer to anchor charts. • Teachers sometimes engage with students in conversations about the books they are reading in order to learn more about their reading processes and reading interests. • Experience is pleasurable and engaging and lots of fun.

If you will recall Nathan's English homework assignment once again, instructional context played an important role in the way that Kim scaffolded Nathan's learning. Had she been able to follow her instincts, Nathan would have had a shared reading experience.

Selecting the instructional context best suited for a lesson is a nuanced and complex process. Instructional context dictates how much work the teacher is going to do and how much work the student is going to do. When we successfully pair readers with the right instructional context for a given text, we maximize the amount of work the students do. When selecting an instructional context, ask yourself: Given a particular text, which instructional context gives students the biggest opportunity to experience productive effort—hard work that results in success rather than frustration?

Optimizing the Benefits of the Gradual Release of Responsibility

In closing this book, we offer you a handful of big ideas that sum up the thinking described throughout *Who's Doing the Work?* These are the takeaways that we want you to hold on to as you explore text with your students during read-aloud, shared reading, guided reading, and independent reading. We have found that holding tight to the following ideas helps nurture eager readers with integrated and efficient reading processes.

Work Across the Gradual Release of Responsibility Should Focus on the Reading Process as Much as Possible

In Chapter 1 of this book, we explore at length a relatively simple way to think about reading process, or the ways that students integrate print and meaning information from a text to construct knowledge. Work across all the instructional contexts should focus on the reading process as much as possible rather than on subskills or isolated strategies. We are not suggesting that you never teach students to infer, predict, and so on explicitly. Rather, students' work needs to be mostly about integrating strategies into their complete reading processes in ways that are authentic and make reading more efficient.

Work Across the Gradual Release of Responsibility Should Begin with the End in Mind

As much as possible, the work in all instructional contexts should support the kinds of independent reading you want students to practice. Do you want students to preview books before they read them? Then model this in read-aloud, practice it in shared reading, observe it in guided reading, and expect students to practice previewing on their own in independent reading. Rather than remind students to preview texts, use anchor charts to support previewing and expect students to look at pictures and read book-jacket blurbs before beginning new books.

Just as important, *don't* practice reading in ways that you do *not* want students to read independently. For example, students will not have introductory summaries to texts when they are reading independently. They need to learn strategies for introducing *themselves* to new texts rather than rely on introductions by teachers. So, instruction across the gradual release of responsibility should teach students *when* to use a strategy, such as previewing a text, as much as how to use it, and you should expect to see students using the strategy independently.

Work Across the Gradual Release of Responsibility Should Be Aligned

Work in one instructional context should support the work in the other instructional contexts. If you are practicing rereading and thinking deeply about the text during read-aloud, don't shift to talking about predicting in isolation during shared reading. The instruction from read-aloud *through* independent reading should be connected in intentional ways. Too often, we see classrooms where, for example, the read-aloud lesson focuses on the main idea whereas guided reading focuses on using context to figure out words and independent reading begins with a mini-lesson on clarifying. We lose the power inherent in the gradual release when we don't connect our instruction across it.

Reading for Meaning Is intrinsically Standards Based

If you find an excellent text and students read it deeply and have discussions exploring what they notice and what the text means, then you are practicing standards-based instruction. You do not have to teach a discrete skill with every lesson! Constructing meaning from text is the purpose of reading and is practice in comprehending. Children who can read and comprehend will score well on tests! We are not opposed to learning targets, but more often than not, reading instruction should focus on reading, not on isolated strategies or skills.

Work Across the Gradual Release of Responsibility Should Include All Four Instructional Contexts

Teachers maximize the effectiveness of the gradual release of responsibility by thoughtfully teaching within all four instructional contexts. Each instructional context—read-aloud, shared reading, guided reading, and independent reading—serves a distinct purpose and contributes to accelerating students' proficiency in increasingly difficult texts. If you leave out shared reading, for example, you skip working with students in texts that they are about to grow into, which would prime them for texts of increased difficulty. If you leave out independent reading, you will not know if your work in the other instructional contexts is transferring to students' independent interactions with texts. You must do them all—read-aloud, shared reading, guided reading, independent reading—with regularity!

Each Instructional Context Across the Gradual Release of Responsibility Is Equally Important and Warrants as Much Instructional Time as the Others

Because all four instructional contexts work together as a whole, none is more important than another. This is why, for example, we encourage teachers who are not teaching shared reading at all but are teaching guided reading every day to supplant some of their guided reading instruction with shared reading. Trends in the field encourage rotating attention among different instructional contexts. When independent reading is popular among educators, it gets daily attention in classrooms; when it is not, it gets little time. But we suggest that you insulate yourself from the waffling that results from reading's politics and set your students up for more success by evenly attending to read-aloud, shared reading, guided reading, and independent reading. Look closely at your instructional schedule and ferret out any favoritism or neglect. To teach all four instructional contexts well, you may find it easier to equally (-ish!) distribute instructional time for each context over the course of a week rather than do a little of each instructional context each day.

Final Thoughts

In *Brown Girl Dreaming,* Jacqueline Woodson (2014) writes,

> When there are many worlds
>
> you can choose the one
>
> you walk into each day. (139)

These words poetically capture what we hope you will take away from both this chapter and this book. Each day that you walk into your classroom, you have many, many choices. Some days you may lean in the direction of conventional instruction, and other days you may lean in the direction of next generation instruction. As always, we encourage you to trust your inner teacher (Burkins and Yaris 2014) and practice the aspects of next generation reading instruction that align with what you believe about teaching and learning. Implementation does not have to be all of one perspective and none of the other.

Your choices about when to use each of the instructional contexts, your decisions about which text to use, and your intentional responses to students' efforts to figure out the tricky parts in a text all contribute to the "world" that nurtures your students' growth and independence as readers. When children inhabit worlds where teachers let them do the work, they learn from their productive effort, become empowered to take charge of their reading lives, and, very often, surprise us with what they can do! As you work to translate the ideas we have presented in this book into your instruction, use this guiding question as your compass: Who's doing the work?

References

Allen, Janet. 2002. *On The Same Page: Shared Reading Beyond the Primary Grades*. Portland, ME: Stenhouse.

Allington, Richard L. 2011. *What Really Matters for Struggling Readers: Designing Research-Based Programs*. New York: Longman.

Allington, Richard L., and Anne McGill-Franzen. 2013. *Summer Reading: Closing the Rich/Poor Reading Achievement Gap*. New York: Teachers College Press.

Alvermann, Donna E., Norman J. Unrau, and Robert B. Ruddell. 2013. *Theoretical Models and Processes of Reading*. Newark, DE: International Reading Association.

Atwell, Nancie. 2007. *The Reading Zone: How to Help Kids Become Skilled, Passionate, Habitual, Critical Readers*. New York: Scholastic.

Avi. 1995. *Poppy*. New York: Orchard Books.

Barnhouse, Dorothy. 2014. *Readers Front and Center: Helping All Students Engage with Complex Texts*. Portland, ME: Stenhouse.

Barnhouse, Dorothy, and Vicki Vinton. 2012. *What Readers Really Do: Teaching the Process of Meaning Making*. Portsmouth, NH: Heinemann.

Beard, Daniel Carter. 2001. *The American Boy's Handy Book: What to Do and How to Do It*. Centennial ed. Rutland, VT: C.E. Tuttle.

Beers, Kylene. 2003. *When Kids Can't Read: What Teachers Can Do.* Portsmouth, NH: Heinemann.

Betts, Emmett A. 1946. *Foundations of Reading Instruction, with Emphasis on Differentiated Guidance.* New York: American Book Company.

Boushey, Gail, and Joan Moser. 2014. *The Daily 5: Fostering Literacy Independence in the Elementary Grades.* 2nd ed. Portland, ME: Stenhouse.

Burkins, Jan Miller, and Melody M. Croft. 2010. *Preventing Misguided Reading: New Strategies for Guided Reading Teachers.* Newark, DE: International Reading Association.

Burkins, Jan Miller, and Kim Yaris. 2014. *Reading Wellness: Lessons in Independence and Proficiency.* Portland, ME: Stenhouse.

Chinery, Michael. 1992. *Rainforest Animals.* New York: Random House.

Clay, Marie M. 1979. *The Early Detection of Reading Difficulties.* 2nd ed. Portsmouth, NH: Heinemann.

_____. 1991. *Becoming Literate.* Portsmouth, NH: Heinemann.

_____. 1994. *Reading Recovery: a Guidebook for Teachers in Training.* Portsmouth, NH: Heinemann.

Collins, Billy. 2002. "Velocity." In *Nine Horses: Poems.* New York: Random House.

Cunningham, Katie Egan. 2015. *Story: Still the Heart of Literacy Learning.* Portland, ME: Stenhouse.

Dahl, Roald. 1964. *Charlie and the Chocolate Factory.* New York: A. A. Knopf.

DiCamillo, Kate. 2013. *Flora and Ulysses.* Somerville, MA: Candlewick.

Dweck, Carol S. 2006. *Mindset: The New Psychology of Success.* New York: Random House.

Evans, Lynette. 2009. *Little Blue Fish.* New York: Scholastic.

Fecho, Bob. 2013. "Globalization, Localization, Uncertainty, and Wobble: Implications for Education." *International Journal for Dialogical Sciences* 7 (1): 115–128.

Ford, Michael P., and Michael F. Opitz. 2008. "Guided Reading: Then and Now." In *An Essential History of Current Reading Practices*, ed. Mary Jo Fresch. Newark, NJ: International Reading Association.

Fountas, Irene C., and Gay Su Pinnell. 1996. *Guided Reading: Good First Teaching for All Children*. Portsmouth, NH: Heinemann.

———. 2015. "Decades of Guided Reading: The Romance and Reality." Presentation at the Annual Convention of the International Literacy Association, St. Louis, Missouri, July 18.

Fullan, Michael. 2013. *Stratosphere: Integrating Technology, Pedagogy, and Change Knowledge*. Don Mills, ON: Pearson.

Gallup. 2014. *State of America's Schools: The Path to Winning Again in Education*. http://products.gallup.com/168380/state-education-report-main-page.aspx.

Gladwell, Malcolm. 2008. *Outliers: The Story of Success*. New York: Little, Brown.

Holdaway, Don. 1979. *The Foundations of Literacy*. Sydney, Australia: Ashton Scholastic.

———. 1980. *Independence in Reading: A Handbook on Individualized Procedures*. Gosford, NSW, Australia: Ashton Scholastic.

Hutchins, Pat. 1968. *Rosie's Walk*. New York: Macmillan.

Johnston, Peter H. 2012. *Opening Minds: Using Language to Change Lives*. Portland, ME: Stenhouse.

Joyce, William. 2012. *The Fantastic Flying Books of Mr. Morris Lessmore*. New York: Atheneum.

Justice, Laura M., Khara L. Pence, Angela R. Beckman, Lori E. Skibbe, and Alice K. Wiggins. 2005. *Scaffolding with Storybooks: A Guide for Enhancing Young Children's Language and Literacy Achievement*. Newark, DE: International Reading Association.

Kinney, Jeff. 2007. *Diary of a Wimpy Kid: A Novel in Cartoons*. New York: Amulet.

Kohn, Alfie. 1993. *Punished by Rewards: The Trouble with Gold Stars, Incentive Plans, A's, Praise, and Other Bribes*. Boston: Houghton Mifflin.

Landon, Kristen. 2010. *The Limit*. New York: Aladdin.

Layne, Steven L. 2015. *In Defense of Read-Aloud: Sustaining Best Practice*. Portland, ME: Stenhouse.

Lionni, Leo. 1968. *The Alphabet Tree*. New York: Random House.

Lyons, Carol A., Gay Su Pinnell, and Diane E. DeFord. 1993. *Partners in Learning: Teachers and Children in Reading Recovery*. New York: Teachers College Press.

Mackinnon, Mairi. 2007. *The Fox and the Stork: Based on a Story by Aesop*. London: Usborne.

McDonnell, Patrick. 2011. *Me . . . Jane*. New York: Little, Brown.

Miller, Donalyn. 2009. *The Book Whisperer: Awakening the Inner Reader in Every Child*. San Francisco: Jossey-Bass.

Mitra, Sugata. 2010. "The Child-driven Education." TEDGlobal. July. http://www.ted.com/talks/sugata_mitra_the_child_driven_education?language=en#t-223423.

Osborne, Mary Pope. 1992. *Dinosaurs Before Dark*. New York: Random House.

Osborne, Will, and Mary Pope Osborne. 2000. *Dinosaurs*. New York: Random House.

Palacio, R. J. 2012. *Wonder*. New York: Random House.

Parkes, Brenda. 2000. *Read It Again! Revisiting Shared Reading*. Portland, ME: Stenhouse.

Pea, Roy D. 2004. "The Social and Technological Dimensions of Scaffolding and Related Theoretical Concepts for Learning, Education, and Human Activity." *Journal of the Learning Sciences* 13(3): 423–451. doi: 10.1207/s15327809jls1303_6.

Pearson, P. David, and Margaret C. Gallagher. 1983. "The Instruction of Reading Comprehension." *Contemporary Educational Psychology* 8(3): 317–344. doi:10.1016/0361-476X(83)90019-X.

Pfizer. 2015. Celebrex Pharmaceutical Warnings. https://www1.pfizerpro. com/hcp/celebrex?source=google&HBX_PK=s_+celebrex+samples&o =78847767|255139986|0&skwid=43700005476052303.

Pilkey, Dav. 1999. *Captain Underpants and the Attack of the Talking Toilets*. New York: Scholastic.

Polacco, Patricia. 1998. *Thank You, Mr. Falker*. New York: Philomel Books.

Price, Susan D. 2001. *Locked In*. South Melbourne, Australia: Nelson Thomson Learning.

Rawls, Wilson. 1961. *Where The Red Fern Grows: The Story of Two Dogs and a Boy*. Garden City, NY: Doubleday.

Rosenblatt, Louise M. 2004. "The Transactional Theory of Reading and Writing." In *Theoretical Models and Processes of Reading,* 5th ed., eds. Robert B. Ruddell and Norman J. Unrau. Newark, DE: International Reading Association.

Rowling, J. K. 1997. *Harry Potter and the Sorcerer's Stone.* New York: Scholastic.

Schlitz, Laura Amy. 2015. *The Hired Girl*. Somerville, MA: Candlewick.

Seligman, Martin E. P., and Steven F. Maier. 1967. "Failure to Escape Traumatic Shock." *Journal of Experimental Psychology* 74(1): 1–9. doi: 10.1037/ h0024514.

Trelease, Jim. 2013. *The Read-Aloud Handbook*. 7th ed. Harmondsworth, UK: Penguin.

Vygotsky, L. S. 1978. *Mind in Society: The Development of Higher Psychological Processes*. Cambridge, MA: Harvard University Press.

Walsh, Bridget A. 2008. "Quantity, Quality, Children's Characteristics, and Vocabulary Learning." *Childhood Education* 84: 163–166.

White, Bailey. 1993. *Mama Makes Up Her Mind: And Other Dangers of Southern Living*. Reading, MA: Addison-Wesley.

White, E. B. 1952. *Charlotte's Web*. New York: HarperCollins.

Winter, Jeanette. 2010. *Biblioburro: A True Story from Colombia*. New York: Beach Lane Books.

Wood, David, Jerome S. Bruner, and Gail Ross. 1976. "The Role of Tutoring in Problem Solving." *Journal of Child Psychology and Psychiatry* 17(2): 89–100.

Woodson, Jacqueline. 2014. *Brown Girl Dreaming*. New York: Random House.

Index

Page numbers followed by *f* and *t* indicate figures and tables.

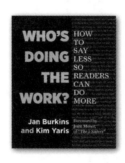